God in Flesh
The biblical evidence that Jesus is God

Peter Denio & Daniel Lawry

Copyright © 2009 Peter Denio and Daniel Lawry

Acknowledgments

Many thanks to Dr. Timothy Christian *(Mid America Baptist Theological Seminary)*, Craig & Meredith Williams *(First Presbyterian of Schenectady, NY)*, Angie Lawry *(Trinity Baptist of Niskayuna, NY)*, John Dalgety *(Faith Baptist of Manchester, NH)*, Evan Mennillo *(Loudonville Community Church of Loudonville, NY)*, Pastor Scott Lawry *(Grace @ Bell Road Presbyterian of Montgomery, AL)*, Andrew Von Gillern *(Harvest Bible Chapel of Gurnee, IL)*, and Brian Merriam *(Bellevue Gospel Chapel of Schenectady, NY)* for the helpful suggestions and time in editing.

✔ Written in easy-to-understand language, while Biblically right on the mark.

✔ Presents the most clear and indisputable passages showing that Jesus is God.

✔ Useful for those who have a fuzzy belief in the deity of Christ but cannot solidly defend it.

✔ Valuable to clearly explain who Jesus really is to Jehovah's Witnesses, Mormons, and members of the various cults.

✔ Each section includes practical applications for various areas of life.

Contents

1

<u>High Stakes</u>

This book is dedicated to the ultimate question. It is the only question that matters. Forget everything until you consider this, because your eternal life or condemnation rests on it. Your answer seals your destiny. It comes down to this: **Is Jesus *created* or *Creator*?**

There is more than a vast difference between the two. If Jesus is merely a created "being," he's not worth our time. He certainly does not have the authority to forgive offenses against the One who is the very standard of morality. He neither has the authority to grant eternal life nor to pronounce sentence on the Day of Judgment. He might have been a wise philosopher, a good teacher, an example of love and sacrifice, but nothing more.

Many cults would agree that Jesus is god, at least according to their definition. You probably could even convince an atheist to say that Jesus is "divine." These days, "god" is a vague term. It has been redefined and no longer has the same force that the Bible attributes to it. Even fuzzier are the words, "divine" or "deity." Have you considered, though, the Bible's claim that Jesus is not only divine, not only god, but the One and Only God, ...THE God?

In your Bible reading you may have noticed that sometimes "Lord" is written "LORD" with all capital letters. This is the translators' way of showing you that the name being translated is "Yahweh." Yahweh is the name that is used *exclusively* for the One True God. It is never applied to anyone else. It never refers to an angel. It never refers to a king, no matter how renowned. It is God's name. This name Yahweh is used around 6500 times in the Bible. If I repeated 6500 times, *"Be to work on time,"* would you suppose that it was important?

The burden of this book is to show passage after passage where Jesus is identified as capital LORD, as Yahweh. It was Jesus who created DNA and magnetism and heat. It was He, along with two angels, who dragged Lot and his family out of Sodom before decimation. It was He who accepted the burnt sacrifice of Sampson's father Manoah. It was He who spoke out of the flaming bush to Moses, the One who rained down the manna, the One whose appearance to Ezekiel caused him to drop in a dead faint for seven days, the One who sent the monster of a fish to swallow Jonah and regurgitate him later, and the One to whom David prayed for strength and aid. We hope that you're thinking, *"Jesus is Him? Is that solidly defendable? I've got to check this out. That sure raises the bar..."*

If this is true, it changes everything. No wonder Stephen was willing to preach the unedited word of God in the face of opposition and danger. No wonder Paul so boldly faced King Agrippa and his court and was willing to be flogged and chained. It changes everything. A teen who understands who Jesus is will be willing to go against the flow at school. When all around him are spewing crude language, watching ungodly movies, making fun of other students, cheating on homework, and indulging in pornography, he'll stand firm. He will hold fast to the truth and be willing to take the heat. A man who sees who Jesus is will act the same at work as in church. His daughter could sneak into the office and hide under his desk for the afternoon and he would not be ashamed at anything he said to his coworkers, on the phone, or typed on email. This guy acts the same whether alone or in a crowd, whether at home or at work, because he knows that someday he's going to face Jesus and that is all that matters.

You can be a follower of Jesus and be wrong in your view about whether you should sprinkle infants or baptize adults. You can be unclear about issues concerning divorce and remarriage. You can be skewed in your end-time chronology. These are all important, but differing views on these things will not condemn you on the Last Day. However, if you are wrong about the identity of Jesus, everything else is dust on the scale.

This might NOT be for you

If you hold that the Bible is the deciding factor in any question or argument, this book is for you. If you don't believe that the Bible is the ultimate authority, thanks for contributing toward our kids' college tuition, but you have picked up the wrong book. Step back and confirm for yourself that the Bible is the very word of God, unique from Genesis to Revelation. For the rest, if you have always wondered if the Bible really says that Jesus is the One and Only God, read on.

This is intended to be standard reading for the Bible school and seminary student, a resource for pastors, and most importantly, easy and interesting reading for the regular Joe. Clarity is a major goal of this book. The chapters are short and self-sufficient in order to be used by small group leaders in churches and college campuses who lead Bible studies about who Jesus is and His great offer.

2

<u>One Maker -</u>
<u>Dirt to DNA to Dinosaurs</u>

You and I can cut, weld, grind, and rivet something together. Don't be fooled though, that's not *"creating."* We can melt down and pour into a mold, extrude it into wire, cut and bend it, and cover it in paint. That's far from *creating*. We merely have the ability to find stuff, combine things, and name it something else. We have to drop a maple or oak and rip into boards, dig something out of the ground, or mix chemicals we find. *Creation* is much different. You and I do not have the ability to create. No human ever has. Creation is <u>out of nothing</u>. It's building with no raw material. Creation is a *God-thing*.

The Bible says that there is **one** Creator. Of course you do not have to be a Bible-reader to know that. Three basics that all should know before graduating from first grade are:

<u>Number 1</u>: **Design means there is a designer.**
<u>Number 2</u>: **Stuff doesn't burst from "non-stuff."**
<u>Number 3</u>: **Information doesn't sprout from non-information.**

The Old Testament says that Yahweh alone is able to do this God-thing. He alone is Creator.

Unlike the company CEO who only oversees the work, Yahweh very directly created. In Job 38-41 Yahweh specifically claims to have made the springs, sea, clouds, lightning, hail, snow, and rain. He Himself created the Pleiades and Orion constellations. The passage says that He specifically created the stork, ostrich, hawk, and eagle, and food for them. He created the dinosaurs. (You can read about the behemoth for yourself in Job 40; it was some kind of massive dinosaur, with a tail like a tree, and is now extinct.) Yahweh created the leviathan, an even more fascinating creature of days gone by. In Isaiah 40, Yahweh said that He Himself measured the earth's water and dirt in His hand. He created the sun and moon and knows each star individually by name:

"Lift your eyes and look to the heavens: Who created all these? He who brings out the starry host one by one, and calls them each by name." *(Isaiah 40:26)*

Yahweh alone created. He did the design, and His mind and hands and muscle got it done. There was no one to help Him. Psalm 89:12 is explicit that He created the North and South. And you've known since you were little what Genesis 1-2 says about light, animals, plants, and man. Yahweh's hands did the construction and gluing and twisting together of the DNA. If there's one thing we know about Yahweh, it is that He is the One Creator. This fact is stamped all over the Old Testament. And there is a huge, a vast, an infinite difference between the Creator and the created.

Now look at how the New Testament describes Jesus:

"For by him all things were created..."
(Colossians 1:16)

You might call this a major clue to his identity. In case you want to pin down exactly what "all things" means, read on:

"...things in heaven and on earth, visible and invisible, whether thrones or powers or rulers or authorities; all things were created by him and for him. He is before all things, and in him all things hold together." *(Col 1:16-17)*

All means all. Every electron orbiting every nucleus, every molecule from one end of the universe to the other, and every rank of spirit creature in heaven was created by Jesus. Verse 17 says that even up to this very day and hour Jesus Himself holds gravity, the laws of radiation, magnetism, optics, centrifugal force, $E=mc^2$, thermodynamics, physics, the travel of sound and light, and whatever other laws there are.

This isn't the only passage. John says the same thing:

> **"Through him <u>all</u> things were made; without him <u>nothing</u> was made that has been made. ... He was in the world, and though the world was made through him, the world did not recognize him."**
> *(John 1:3,10)*

Again, he clarifies what "all things" is so that you do not have any doubt. (Compare the first line of John to the first line of Genesis and you'll again see the point.) Jesus did the thing which is exclusively a *God-thing*. Is this at odds with the Old Testament? Surely not. The New Testament and Old Testament never conflict, since the same author is the One Mind behind them both.

The solution is evident. The Bible says that Yahweh is the One Maker, while it also says that Jesus is the One Maker. There is no way around it: Yahweh is the One who lowered Himself to become a man, to pay the terrible moral price that you owe. So, who was jeered and spit in the face? Whose blood was spattered along the streets of Jerusalem? It puts a different perspective on the enormity of the price that was paid for you doesn't it? And what you owe Him.

The next section shows that Yahweh is the only One deserving of worship. Receiving worship, like being the Creator, is exclusively a *God-thing*, and the implication is the same.

3

<u>One Worthy of Worship</u>

Rick geared up for Valentine's Day. He bought his wife a beautiful bouquet of roses to go with a box of Lindt chocolates. It was the best Valentine's Day ever! But trouble is right at his heels. At the end of the month, Rick's wife was floored when she received the credit card bill. In the days leading up to February 14, Rick had spent $1800 at Val's Floral shop! When she showed him the card statement and asked him how he had amassed such a huge bill, he explained to her, that after he bought the bouquet for her, he got the same bouquet for some ladies at work, including Wendy, Kate, Jillian, Carolyn, Sarah, Gayle, Cathy...

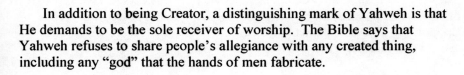

In addition to the economic ramifications of his purchase, Rick's wife is no longer gratified with her gift. She's burning angry. Why? There is only one who deserves such a gift from Rick: *his wife*.

In addition to being Creator, a distinguishing mark of Yahweh is that He demands to be the sole receiver of worship. The Bible says that Yahweh refuses to share people's allegiance with any created thing, including any "god" that the hands of men fabricate.

In the ancient world, it was normal to believe in many gods and their girlfriends. One might give allegiance to a national deity, pay homage to a tribal god, or even have a household god. No one had absolute allegiance to any one god. To cover your bases sufficiently, you would offer sacrifice and worship to multiple gods. It was like betting on multiple horses. The more horses you place a bet on, the higher the probability that one will be a winner. In the same way, someone in the ancient world would offer worship to many gods in order to ensure their family's safety and protection.

You can see how much of an oddball a one-God man would be in such a world. Yet, Yahweh demands that His followers are radically counter-cultural:

"You shall have no other gods before me." *(Exodus 20:3)*

"Do not worship any other god, for the LORD, whose name is Jealous, is a jealous God." *(Exodus 34:14)*

"Do not invoke the names of their gods or swear by them. You must not serve them or bow down to them." *(Joshua 23:7)*

"Will you ...follow other gods ... and then come and stand before me in this house, which bears my Name, and say, 'We are safe' ?"
(Jeremiah 7:9-10)

This is stamped all over Scripture: *Yahweh demands exclusive worship. He does not want to share it with anyone.*

Has this changed in the New Testament? Many walk around with the idea that God in the Old Testament was harsh, and everything was all judgment. They feel that in the New Testament, God has really started to mellow out, and now He's all love, love, love. The fact is that God's nature has not, and does not, change. In the previous chapter, we saw that the New Testament authors continued believing that Yahweh was THE Creator. The New Testament also continued the Old Testament's solid affirmation that only Yahweh deserves worship:

"Jesus said to him, 'Away from me, Satan! For it is written: 'Worship the Lord your God, and serve *him only*.'" *(Matthew 4:10)*

"So he will fall down and worship God, exclaiming, 'God is really among you!'" *(1 Corinthians 14:25)*

"Therefore, since we are receiving a kingdom that cannot be shaken, let us be thankful, and so worship God acceptably with reverence and awe." *(Hebrews 12:28)*

"At this I fell at his feet to worship him (the angel). But he said to me, *'Do not do it! I am a fellow servant with you and with your brothers who hold to the testimony of Jesus. Worship God! For the testimony of Jesus is the spirit of prophecy.'"* *(Revelation 19:10)*

As you can see, the New Testament continues the demand to *exclusively* worship Yahweh. Like the previous chapter, though, there is something eye opening when it comes to worshipping Him. Let's look at Revelation 4-5 as an example. This passage guarantees that every man and woman and angel will worship Jesus Himself, not only on earth, but in the very center throne room of the universe.

Jesus is Greater Than You Think
Revelation 4-5

John sees a glimpse of the terrifying and overwhelming throne room of Glory and the One firmly seated there. This is He who exists eternally. This is the One True God: *"Holy, holy, holy is the Lord God Almighty, who was, and is, and is to come." (Revelation 4:8)* John was terrified at the radiance and shaking and rumblings and lightning — felt like he was going to throw up and black out.

He then noticed something he had not at first: The One on the throne was holding something in His right hand. Then there's a cosmic shout:

"And I saw a mighty angel proclaiming in a loud voice, *'Who is worthy to break the seals and open the scroll?'* " *(Rev 5:2)*

The challenge is proclaimed throughout every expanse, every region, and every corner of the universe. It's yelled with a mighty yell across the earth, under the earth, and through the heavens. *Who is worthy? Is there anyone worthy? If you think you measure up, step forward! Approach the Mighty One, the Judge, the Creator. Who thinks he measures up?*

The echoing of the angel's words tapers off and there is utter absolute silence. Dead silence. Did any supposed "saints" dare come forward? Mary? Mohammed? The mighty archangel Michael? No, it would require an ability greater than any created being to approach the arcing, thundering throne of the Creator. Sweat beaded up on John's face, and the rough fisherman bawled like a baby:

"But no one in heaven or on earth or under the earth could open the scroll or even look inside it. I wept and wept because no one was found who was worthy to open the scroll or look inside."
(Rev 5:3-4)

John felt naked in the presence of the Mighty One. He realized that he was in deep trouble. Lying is not just against your parents or employer. That's the least of it. It's against the One whose very nature sets the standard of truth. Self-centeredness, crude language, abortion, and cheating are not just against tradition or culture – they are in direct defiance to the Creator Himself. And He is the Greatest One there is to defy. John cried and cried as he faced the Judge. He knew the gavel was coming down, and it was in the hand of the Greatest Judge there is to face.

But then, the armies of heaven stir. Someone was approaching, someone of unfathomable, unimaginable, inconceivable greatness:

"Then one of the elders said to me, *'Do not weep! See, the Lion of the tribe of Judah, the Root of David, has triumphed. He is able to open the scroll and its seven seals.'" *(Rev 5:5)*

"The lion"... some sort of king? But what mere king is worthy? "The root"... someone related to King David, but before King David's time? John then sees a lamb, looking as if had been slaughtered and then raised to life.

If you were a Jew reading this back then, mention of the "lamb" would really mean something to you. When you violated God's law, the law required you to bring a lamb to the temple, and with your own hands grasp the knife and cut its throat (Lev 4:27-29). The blood on your hands was a gruesome reminder that you were wicked guilty in the sight of the Holy One. He is just, and payment has to be made. Obviously an animal can't pay for a man, but the blood on your hands reminded you of your desperate need of a Savior.

This is no mere lamb in the "temple" of heaven who dares to approach the throne. In days past, John the Baptist was down in the river teaching about facing God. Then he stopped. His eyes opened wide, and his face lit up, and the crowds turned to see who he was pointing at. **"Look, the lamb of God who takes away the sin of the world!"** (John 1:29) He was pointing to Jesus. In fact, all those sacrificed lambs in Old Testament days pointed to Jesus.

Here in Revelation Jesus showed himself looking like a cut-up lamb to drive home to John and to you the payment that he made. The innocent paid for the guilty. His death is more significant than you think. When he took the scroll, look what happened:

"And when he had taken it, the four living creatures and the twenty-four elders fell down before the Lamb." *(Rev 5:8)*

The *"Holy, Holy, Holy"* song, the worship that was directed from immeasurable time past to the Creator, to Yahweh Himself, fell silent! This is major. The elders and creatures turn, and then they fall down. Before whom? Look:

"And they sang a new song: *'You are worthy to take the scroll and to open its seals, because you were slain, and with your blood you purchased men for God from every tribe and language and people and nation. You have made them to be a kingdom and priests to serve our God, and they will reign on the earth.'* **"** *(Rev 5:9-10)*

It's unthinkable that the Creator would have allowed this. Look what they're doing: They're <u>worshipping</u> Jesus, and this is happening even in the very throne room, right under the very nose of God Himself! How would the Almighty allow such blasphemy? How could He allow the utmost violation of the laws of right and wrong in His fullest presence?

"Then I looked and heard the voice of many angels, numbering thousands upon thousands, and ten thousand times ten thousand. *(What do you think God is trying to get at?)* **They encircled the throne and the living creatures and the elders. In a loud voice they sang:** *'Worthy is the Lamb* (Who?!), *who was slain, to receive power and wealth and wisdom and strength and honor and glory and praise!'* **"** *(Rev 5:11-12)*

In unison, <u>**all**</u> the angels thunder to Jesus — angels everywhere in the universe, crowding on all sides like in a great stadium. **"Glory and honor and power"** are exactly the same words as Revelation 4:11, which describe the One on the throne, the Creator Himself. Here, they are directed to Jesus. But there is *more* ascribed to Jesus, **"power and wealth and wisdom"** (the honors are piled on like cord wood) **"and strength and honor"** (it keeps coming...) **"and glory and praise!"** Consider this. If the Creator's worthiness, power, awesomeness, and authority is at ceiling level (of course His "level" is way beyond even that) then what would be the highest level attainable of one who is not the Creator? Halfway up? An inch above the floor? Obviously, the answer is in the dirt, because there is an infinite difference between the Creator and the created.

Here is the only conclusion: Jesus is no mere angel or created being. It says here in Revelation that all angels worship Jesus. Jesus is worthy, He has measured up, because He IS the Creator, He IS the Holy One. You say, *"Well how can Jesus take the scroll from God if He is God?"* Answer this first: Do you suppose that it is possible for the Almighty to be in two places at the same time? Not partially, but *fully* in two places at once? We have to answer yes (Psalm 139 for example), and that is what is happening here.

John keeps looking:

> **"Then I heard every creature in heaven and on earth and under the earth and on the sea, and all that is in them, singing:** *'To him who sits on the throne and to the Lamb be praise and honor and glory and power, for ever and ever!'* **"** *(Rev 5:13)*

You don't have to be too good at math to know what these two horizontal bars mean:

What's clear in vs. 13 is that all creation is worshipping both the "One on the throne" and Jesus EQUALLY. This only makes sense when realizing that Jesus is Yahweh.

Look what the creatures declare:

> **"The four living creatures said, *'Amen,'* and the elders fell down and worshiped."** *(Rev 5:14)*

"Amen" comes from a Hebrew word which means "truth." It's giving the thumbs up. They're saying, *"This is true, we agree, it is so."* What exactly are they saying is true? The fact that was just acknowledged, admitted, and declared by every creature, every created thing. The fact that it is right to worship Jesus equally to the One on the throne.

We are left with the same line of reasoning as in the previous chapter. From the passages above, one can be confident that the writers of the New Testament, who were the earliest Christians and the eyewitnesses to Jesus' life and ministry, believed that Jesus was Yahweh in the flesh. This is the clearest and most logical conclusion.

At this point, one who holds to a different view must accept the burden of proof and make his strongest case. In this book, we have not randomly selected obscure passages whose interpretation could go any of multiple ways. The only other possibility is that the New  Testament authors had abandoned their dearly held and fiercely defended beliefs and adopted some form of polytheism. No one is going to buy that.

Rick (that dope at the beginning of this chapter) made a terrible and costly mistake in offering flowers to others besides his wife. Will you, like Rick, offer your service, devotion, and time to one who is undeserving? An angel? A dead saint? A job? Self? Your possessions? If so, consequences are surely on your heels. Or will you offer your life fully to the One who was slain for you, the only worthy recipient of praise and worship, Jesus, Yahweh Himself in the flesh?

The Appendix lists a number of occasions when Jesus solidified His claim to be Yahweh by accepting worship while on earth. This next section will highlight one.

The Commended Confession
John 20:24-31

With his own eyes Thomas saw the blood staining the dirt along the road. He saw someone beaten so badly that he did not even look like a man. He should not have been still living. Forget the tame pictures that artists dream up. He saw the flesh hanging and blood running down and pooled in the dirt at the base of the cross. When the spear cut in, he knew the surge of water separated from the blood meant death had undeniably already come. You would have brushed off the others in the same way that he did:

"Now Thomas (called Didymus), one of the Twelve, was not with the disciples when Jesus came. So the other disciples told him, *'We have seen the Lord!'* But he said to them, *'Unless I see the nail marks in his hands and put my finger where the nails were, and put my hand into his side, I will not believe it.'* "

(John 20:24-25)

He is in disbelief. Hope is lost. So much for the kingdom of God. *Get over it — we were fooled by a counterfeit.* But a week later:

"A week later his disciples were in the house again, and Thomas was with them. Though the doors were locked, Jesus came and stood among them." *(John 20:26)*

Adrenaline surge. Terror. You would react the same way if you heard a noise, looked up from your book, and all of a sudden found you were not alone. The disciples tensed, shrunk back, reached for their weapons, yelled out. Jesus, however, immediately gives some comforting words:

"Peace be with you!" *(John 20:26)*

Jesus scans the faces in the room, John, Matthew, Andrew. He homes in on one face in particular. Eye to eye. You can see Thomas thinking, "Oh, man. This can't be."

"Then he said to Thomas, *'Put your finger here; see my hands. Reach out your hand and put it into my side. Stop doubting and believe.'* " *(John 20:27)*

Up to that point, Thomas had been in a state of disbelief. In case you had any doubt, Jesus confirms it. Then:

"Thomas said to him, *'My Lord and my God!'* " *(John 20:28)*

Some have figured that this was a mere cry of surprise or astonishment, like using a swear word when someone backs out in front of you. This doesn't hold water, though. In the case of surprise, an exclamation is usually only a syllable or two. This was certainly an intentional act on Thomas' part.

Thomas didn't just say, "My Lord and my God." He addresses his statement to Jesus himself, **"Thomas said TO him."** If it were an exclamation of surprise, it would not be addressed to Jesus or anyone in particular. It would be spoken to the air.

Something else should jump out at you. Jesus **did not correct** Thomas or scold him for using any improper language. If Jesus was God Himself in the flesh, would it not seem odd that he ignores the blatant violation of the third command to his very face, and this offense by one of his closest disciples?

"You shall not misuse the name of the LORD your God, for the LORD will not hold anyone guiltless who misuses his name."
(Exodus 20:7)

It is illogical to think that he would not have rebuked Thomas.

Here is the main reason that we know that Thomas' words were intentional, that he knew exactly what he was saying, and that they were a true statement of belief: No pious or reverent man, or even an angel, would have allowed or accepted or consented being called "Lord and God." Try addressing your pastor that way and see what happens.

Look how Paul violently reacts when treated that way:

> **"The priest of Zeus, whose temple was just outside the city, brought bulls and wreaths to the city gates because he and the crowd wanted to offer sacrifices to them. But when the apostles Barnabas and Paul heard of this, they tore their clothes and rushed out into the crowd, shouting:** *'Men, why are you doing this? We too are only men, human like you.'* **"** *(Acts 14:13-15)*

Look how an angel intensely reacts when treated that way:

> **"I, John, am the one who heard and saw these things. And when I had heard and seen them, I fell down to worship at the feet of the angel who had been showing them to me. But he said to me,** *'Do not do it! I am a fellow servant with you and with your brothers the prophets and of all who keep the words of this book. Worship God!'* **"** *(Rev 22:8-9)*

Look how Peter made Cornelius get up right away:

> **"As Peter entered the house, Cornelius met him and fell at his feet in reverence. But Peter made him get up.** *'Stand up,' he said, 'I am only a man myself.'* **"** *(Acts 10:25-26)*

But, look how Jesus reacts to Thomas' declaration:

> **"Then Jesus told him,** *'Because you have seen me, you have believed; blessed are those who have not seen and yet have believed.'* **"** *(John 20:29)*

After Thomas' words, the first thing out of Jesus' mouth is to immediately <u>commend</u> Him. When I (Dan) was at Maple Avenue Elementary School in Claremont, NH, we got report cards four times per year. The lowest grade was **NI**, "needs improvement." Those are the ones you didn't rush to show mom and dad. Not much better was **S-**, "less than satisfactory." Then **S, S+**, and the top grade was a **C**, meaning "commendable." Here, Jesus <u>commends</u> Thomas. He gives him the top grade. What was the evidence of his believing? How did Jesus know this for certain to be true? It's obvious: It was the statement Thomas just made. Thomas now believed that Jesus was raised and therefore concluded that Jesus was Lord and God.

If this were a mere cry of surprise, what proof was it that Thomas believed? None at all. Before this he doubted. Now he believed and declared so by acknowledging that that Jesus was his Lord and his God. If Thomas' exclamation was a mere act of profanity, do you think that Jesus would have <u>commended</u> him for taking the name of the Lord his God in vain?

John then tells us his purpose for writing:

> **"Jesus did many other miraculous signs in the presence of his disciples, which are not recorded in this book. But these are written that you may believe that Jesus is the Christ, the Son of God, and that by believing you may have life in his name."**
> *(John 20:30-31)*

"Son of God" means, *"God Himself come down in the flesh."* (Chapter 6 shows evidence of this.) It does not mean anything less than God Himself, and that is the reason that "you may have life in his name." We hope that you also will come to realize that Jesus is God, Yahweh Himself, so that you also may have this life.

4

Can You Hear Me Now?

There are a number of times in which Jesus either claims to be Yahweh or the New Testament authors state that fact by quoting the Old Testament. We have chosen these "Top 10" clearest passages to highlight. In this first case, Jesus was nearly murdered for saying it.

No Wonder They Wanted to Stone Him
(John 8 & Exodus 3)

The quiet darkness is broken. He looks around. *Something's up around here. Is someone trying to intimidate me? ...And how on earth is that thing not burning up?*

"So Moses thought, 'I will go over and see this strange sight — why the bush does not burn up.' When the LORD saw that he had gone over to look, God called to him from within the bush, *'Moses! Moses!'* And Moses said, 'Here I am.' 'Do not come any closer,' God said. 'Take off your sandals, for the place where you are standing is holy ground.' Then he said, 'I am the God of your father, the God of Abraham, the God of Isaac and the God of Jacob.'

"At this, Moses hid his face, because he was afraid to look at God. The LORD said, 'I have indeed seen the misery of my people in Egypt. I have heard them crying out because of their slave drivers, and I am concerned about their suffering. ...So now, go. I am sending you to Pharaoh to bring my people the Israelites out of Egypt.' " *(Ex 3:-10)*

His mind raced. *Who is this speaking? Is it Re, the sun god? Could it be Nut, the sky goddess? Shu, god of the wind? Heqt, the god of resurrection, or Seth, or Osiris, or Imhotep, or ...?* Moses knows the first question the leaders will ask him, and no doubt he himself had the same question. He had grown up in pagan Egypt, was adopted by an Egyptian, went to public schools, and was indoctrinated by public broadcasting. He was taught that the various gods oversee the different parts of nature. Yes, he had some good influence, but he also had doubts. *Which deity in particular is speaking? What should I tell the leaders?*

> "Moses said to God, 'Suppose I go to the Israelites and say to them, *The God of your fathers has sent me to you,* and they ask me, *What is his name?* Then what shall I tell them?' God said to Moses, *'I AM WHO I AM. This is what you are to say to the Israelites: 'I AM has sent me to you.'* " *(Ex 3:13-14)*

"I am" sent me? That's sounds weird, doesn't it? I mean, what kind of name is that? That's weird English, and it's weird Hebrew, too. The Voice from the burning bush took the verb, "to be" or "to exist" and adjusted it to suit His purpose. He is using this verb as a proper noun. He is using it as a name. The LORD continues:

> "God also said to Moses, 'Say to the Israelites, *'The LORD, the God of your fathers — the God of Abraham, the God of Isaac and the God of Jacob — has sent me to you.'* This is my name forever, the name by which I am to be remembered from generation to generation.' " *(Ex 3:15)*

In verse 14, when God talks about Himself, He calls Himself, "I AM." It's in the first person (how you refer to yourself). In verse 15, when we refer to Him, the name is changed to "HE IS," the third person (how you refer to someone else). Most English versions put down LORD instead of HE IS. Here's why: From ancient days, the Jews avoided saying this name. It was too holy, too reverent, too awesome a name. When they were discussing Him or reading the Scriptures out loud and came to this name, they would substitute another more generic word for "lord" or "master." This continues even today. Most English translations continue to use LORD instead of Yahweh, out of respect for the name. The capital letters, though, are the clue that the name is Yahweh.

Many years after the bush and plagues and Exodus, Jesus collided with the Jews in the temple courts. The conversation was heating up as Jesus was raising the bar of who he was notch by notch. The Jews are starting to boil:

"At this the Jews exclaimed, 'Now we know that you are demon-possessed! Abraham died and so did the prophets, yet you say that if anyone keeps your word, he will never taste death. Are you greater than our father Abraham? He died, and so did the prophets. Who do you think you are?' " *(John 8:52-53)*

They are disgusted. Although even the greatest prophets have gone to the grave, Jesus is saying that He can keep His followers from dying! "Who does this fool think he is?" Abraham lived in 2000 BC, 2000 years prior to this conversation. That's ancient history.

"Jesus replied, 'If I glorify myself, my glory means nothing. My Father, whom you claim as your God, is the one who glorifies me. Though you do not know him, I know him. If I said I did not, I would be a liar like you, but I do know him and keep his word. Your father Abraham rejoiced at the thought of seeing my day; he saw it and was glad.' *'You are not yet fifty years old,'* the Jews said to him, *'and you have seen Abraham!'* "

(John 8:54-57)

They say, "You're out of your mind! Abraham's bones dried up 2000 years ago." And now Jesus declares something which was throwing a match on gasoline:

"I tell you the truth," Jesus answered, "before Abraham was born, I am!" *(John 8:58)*

This also sounds weird doesn't it? It's weird both in our language and in theirs. It is just as weird as the Exodus 3 passage. If he were claiming to be an angel or spirit being, he would have said, "Before Abraham was born, I **was**."

They certainly knew what he meant. Look at their violent reaction. They wanted his blood, and they would have gotten it if Jesus had not somehow miraculously slipped away:

"At this, they picked up stones to stone him, but Jesus hid himself, slipping away from the temple grounds." *(John 8:59)*

Why were they so upset? Are they like high school English teachers who demand perfect grammar? What had Jesus said that provoked such an intense murderous response? He had obviously used the unspeakable Name, the Name that was revealed at the burning bush. The Name never applied to anyone except Yahweh. And Jesus applied The Name to himself. They knew what Jesus was saying. He was not claiming to know *about* the LORD, or be only a messenger *from* the LORD, or to be *like* the LORD. They understood very clearly that Jesus was claiming to be Yahweh and they responded.

If Jesus thought that his words were misunderstood, he would have immediately corrected them. Can you imagine a truly God-fearing man saying something that led others to believe he was actually God Almighty and not immediately waving his hands and crying out, *"NO! Hold on – back up – you took me wrong!"* Jesus did not correct them, though, because they heard correctly.

If you are a follower of the Lord Jesus, let us determine to live wholeheartedly for Him from this point onward, no turning back, no matter the cost. All that is done apart from Jesus is chasing the wind. Who are we talking about here anyway?

The Ultimate Claim
(Revelation 22:13 & Isaiah 44:6)

Isaiah 44-46 repeats like a broken record. Over and over, Yahweh (the LORD) declares that there is only One True God and He is Him:

> **"This is what the LORD says...I am the first and I am the last; apart from me there is no God."** *(Isaiah 44:6)*
> **"Is there any God besides me?**
> **No, there is no other Rock; I know not one."** *(44:8)*
> **"I am the LORD, who has made all things, who alone stretched out the heavens, who spread out the earth by myself."** *(44:24)*

He's not stopping yet...

> **"I am the LORD, and there is no other;**
> **apart from me there is no God."** *(45:5)*
> **"I am the LORD, and there is no other."** *(45:6)*
> **"I am the LORD, and there is no other."** *(45:18)*

He keeps pressing it...

> **"And there is no God apart from me, a righteous God and a Savior; there is none but me."** *(45:21)*
> **"...for I am God, and there is no other."** *(45:22)*
> **"To whom will you compare me or count me equal?"** *(46:5)*
> **"I am God, and there is no other; I am God,**
> **and there is none like me."** *(46:8-9)*

It's hard to miss the point. The sound track is certainly not broken: the fact is that the LORD doesn't want you to miss it! Look in particular at Isaiah 44:6. This is the heart of it, the bottom line:

> **"This is what the LORD (Yahweh) says — Israel's King and Redeemer, the LORD Almighty: I am the first and I am the last; apart from me there is no God."** *(Isaiah 44:6)*

Yahweh claims to be the First and the Last. We should have a good idea what this means by the surrounding verses, but we don't have to guess, since it's defined in the very next sentence, "apart from me there is no God." "I am the first and I am the last" means that there is no one greater. All others are fakes, counterfeits, and idols. This obviously fits with the theme of these couple of chapters in Isaiah.

This is a major claim. It's more than that – it is an exclusive claim. Yahweh is claiming to be *The Greatest*. Only One who knows everything (not only your deeds, but even your secret thoughts and motivations), only One who can be simultaneously at every point in the extent and breadth of the universe, and only One who is all-powerfully in control of everything can be The Greatest. "The First and The Last" is surely an appropriate title for the True God. He is the Creator, while all else is merely created. Romans 1:25 shows the infinite difference between the two and condemns worshipping and serving anyone but the Creator:

> **"They exchanged the truth of God for a lie, and worshiped and served <u>created things rather than the Creator</u> — who is forever praised. Amen. Because of this, God gave them over to shameful lusts..."** *(Romans 1:25-26)*

Now look at the very end of the Bible:

> **"Behold, I am coming soon! My reward is with me, and I will give to everyone according to what he has done. <u>I am the Alpha and the Omega, the First and the Last, the Beginning and the End. ...I, Jesus</u>, have sent my angel to give you this testimony for the churches. I am the Root and the Offspring of David, and the bright Morning Star."** *(Revelation 22:13, 16)*

It's like the words of verse 13 are blinking on the paper:

> **"I am the Alpha and the Omega, the First and the Last, the Beginning and the End."** *(Rev 22:13)*

We don't have to guess who is speaking, since the verse right before this is spoken by Jesus. Jesus identifies Himself again a few verses afterward:

"I, Jesus, have sent my angel..." *(Rev 22:16)*

You can see for yourself who is making this exclusive "first and last" claim. But Jesus seems to want to nail this down. He tags on that He is the "Alpha and Omega." The New Testament is written in Greek - *Alpha* is the first letter of the Greek alphabet and *Omega* is the last. So He's saying, *"I am the A to Z."* And He goes even further, so that there is no mistaking and to remove all doubt, by also declaring that He is the Beginning and the End.

Look back at Revelation 22:13. If Jesus is merely a created spirit or a prophet, would He make such a claim? It would be unthinkable. It would be the ultimate blasphemy. Even the greatest created angel is nothing compared to the LORD, since the LORD holds together the very stuff of which an angel is made.

How many "Greatests" are there? It makes no sense for Jesus to make this ultimate and exclusive claim about Himself, unless Jesus IS the one and only God, and NOT merely a created being. Jesus hasn't hijacked the word of God. Jesus is the One who spoke not only in Revelation 22, but also in Isaiah 44-45. Jesus is Yahweh. That is the only logical conclusion.

Today, our country's laws are changing. Pastor, if you preach on passages addressing homosexuality (Romans 1:18-32), you may be labeled as a bigot and you risk getting charged with a hate crime. Your church's tax exempt status can be stripped away. Pastor, count the cost, but you have an obligation to teach the word of Jesus. All of it. Concerning divorce and remarriage, no matter that it is the unpopular view. Concerning abortion. Concerning gambling. Concerning debt. Concerning love of possessions. You have an obligation to Him, not the IRS, and not even to your church folks, because Jesus is The Greatest. Are you willing to lose your tax exempt status in order to preach the whole Bible, in order to publically call political leaders to account for their immoral actions, as did John the Baptist, as did Paul, as did the prophets of old? Pastor, are you willing to follow the One who is The Greatest, the One who said, "teaching them to obey <u>everything</u> I have commanded you"?

Isaiah has much more to say about this issue. Let's stay with Isaiah for a bit more.

Can You Hear Me Now?
(Philippians 2:10-11 & Isaiah 45:23)

When I (Dan) was 15, my Uncle Paul and Grampie Prosser had their ham radio licenses and encouraged me to try for my own. I studied how to wire up circuits, build antennas, and use different radios. I spent hours learning Morse Code. When I got my license, my real interest was Morse. I stuffed my small bedroom closet with wires, radios, meters, maps, and telegraph key, and strung long wire antennas out my window to various trees.

Hearing code takes concentration. There's fading and pops and tones and garbage on nearby frequencies. There is a constant "chshshshsh." I hovered over the radio and tweaked the knobs to hear guys in Europe, Brazil, Timbuktu, and even the foreign country of Vermont. When I missed a letter, I could sometimes fill it in by figuring out what the word should be. My radio had filters, and sometimes they helped to muffle the noise but often also squashed the guy I was trying to hear. The worst was if the guy had a "poor hand," which meant the spacing of his dots and dashes was inconsistent.

The LORD's message here in Isaiah isn't hard to understand like Morse code. And there's no static or interference or fading. And His "hand" surely isn't poor! When Isaiah wrote this, the country was sliding out of control. You could count on one hand the number of people who cared anything at all about the LORD. Idolatry was *the thing*, and it was growing like fertilized weeds. In Isaiah 44-45, God blasts a message.

Over and over, the message is: The LORD is the only God. The LORD is the standard. Only what the LORD says will happen. All other supposed gods are counterfeits and idols. The LORD is the only Creator. The LORD is THE God, the

Only God. (If you want to read the pile of passages, look at the previous section, *The Ultimate Claim*.) When the Bible says something once, it is important and we take it seriously. When it says something twice, we really pay attention. But in Isaiah 44 and 45, you get the picture that the LORD's hands are cupped to his mouth, *"Can you hear me now?"*

Isaiah 45:22-23 is the main crux of the deal. It starts, **"...for I am God, and there is no other."** *(Isaiah 45:22)*

Who is speaking in this verse? That is a no-brainer. The LORD. The word LORD is capitalized, and remember that this is no accident. This is the clue used in most English versions of the Bible that this is a particular Hebrew word. Four consonants: יהוה. This word was so reverenced by devout Jews that they <u>never</u> spoke it out loud. They still do not. It might have sounded like "Yahweh." Some people today pronounce it Jehovah (although there isn't a "J" sound in Hebrew). This Hebrew word is a form of the verb "to be," and it means, *"The Being One"* or *"He is"* or *"The One Who Is, Who Was, and Who Is to Come"* or *"The Always-Existing One."* It's the name that the One True God gave for Himself. It is certainly a fitting name. Who else can measure up to such a name? The LORD says:

"for I am God, and there is no other. By myself I have sworn, my mouth has uttered in all integrity a word that will not be revoked" *(Isaiah 45:22-23)*

This is saying that what He is about to declare, He will never take back. What He says will be done. It will be impossible to change, irreversible.

This is quite weird. Is it even possible for God to lie? Truth is inseparable from His very nature, like water is wet. But here, the LORD is making a promise, even more than that, the LORD is actually taking an oath. He's taking the stand and raising His right hand. To swear means to confess or to take an oath. You don't get anything more serious than God taking an oath. The word for swear is the Hebrew word "sheva." It's a word that sounds about the same in Hebrew as in English. It's the number seven, but as a verb. So the LORD is saying, *"I seven myself. I declare it over and over... I declare it seven times."* Man, what is He about to say that could be so important that He is going to such an extent?

Men take oaths and use the name of someone higher to confirm what they say is true. But by whom can the LORD take an oath? Who is higher than Him? So since there is no one higher, He makes it by Himself: **"By myself I have sworn"** (vs. 23). In other words, He is saying, *"In the most serious of words, beyond any doubt, you can bank on this, as certainly as the sun comes up at dawn, as certainly as water freezes as 32 degrees, as certainly as hot air rises — none of these are as certain as what I'm trying to get across to you... As certainly as I exist!...(Can you hear me now?)"* And here is the oath:

"Before me every knee will bow; by me every tongue will swear." *(Isaiah 45:2)*

The LORD, Yahweh, the Being One, the Existing One, says that as surely as He exists, there will come a day when all on the face of the earth will bow down to Him and confess and acknowledge that He alone is the true God, and submit to Him alone and fully. It's referring to the old days of people swearing an oath of total allegiance and service to a king.

Out of all who had read these words, Paul understood it more than anyone. As a top Pharisee, Paul was the most devout of Jews and probably had all 66 chapters of Isaiah memorized. Now here's the point of the matter. Look what Paul declares in Philippians 2:10:

"...at the name of Jesus every knee should bow, (now in case you're wondering what "every" means, let's clarify...) **in heaven and on earth and under the earth, and every tongue confess that <u>Jesus Christ</u> is Lord, to the glory of God the Father."**
(Philippians 2:10-11)

Recognize the quote from Isaiah 45:23?:

"Before me every knee will bow; by me every tongue will swear."
(Isaiah 45:23)

No question, Paul is quoting from Isaiah. He is using the same exact verbs that Isaiah 45:23 uses in the Greek Old Testament for "bow" and "swear/confess." **However, there is a most incredible substitution.** The main character, the speaker, the "me" in Isaiah 45:23, Yahweh Himself, is replaced with another name.

Paul identifies Jesus as Yahweh. He is saying <u>Jesus</u> is the One who swore the oath. Since there was no one higher, <u>Jesus</u> made the oath by Himself. <u>Jesus</u> made the oath that is impossible to be changed or revoked. He's saying <u>Jesus</u> is the Being One, the Existing One, the Creator, the One and Only God, God in the flesh. And here is the three word crux of it: <u>Jesus is Yahweh.</u> Philippians 2:10-11 says that there will be a day when all, whether living in Israel or our town, whether angel or human, whether dead or alive, whether living in BC or AD, Christian or not, willingly or not, will bow down to Jesus and acknowledge Him as the greatest sovereign master and the Only God, the LORD, Yahweh Himself. For those who are not followers of Jesus, this will be a terrifying day. In horror and shame they will recognize who Jesus is and realize the fair consequence of being pronounced guilty with eternal condemnation. On this day all that is now unjust will be made just. All that is now twisted will be made straight. But for the follower of Jesus, this will be the greatest day; we already love Him and willingly confess that He is the only God.

Remember the commercial with the *"Can you hear me now"* man? He was the test man for Verizon Wireless cell phones. With his Verizon cell phone, he would roam the country through wheat fields, across snowy mountains, through airports, along highways, all sorts of crazy places, and at each place take out his cell phone and make a call, *"Can you hear me now?"* and give a slight smile and say, *"Good."* In a bowling alley, through people's backyards, *"Can you hear me now? ...Good."* God is going out of His way, He's determined here in His Bible to get this across to you. Jesus is of no comparison to the rest. He's the real deal. He has the same names as God, same characteristics as God, does things only God can do, receives worship as only God deserves. <u>Jesus is Yahweh, the Eternal One.</u>

These two passages would be excellent to share with a Jehovah's Witness. What more can you ask for? You want to witness for Jesus, and there are people who are actually coming to your front door and want to talk about it! Now write down Isaiah 45:23 and Philippians 2:10 in the cover of your Bible so that you'll remember in the heat of the moment. They won't read this book or anything you give them, since their Watchtower Society doesn't allow it. But they will listen to you, and the Lord Jesus will give you the words to say at the right time. Do not argue or get heated. Your only job is to declare the Word faithfully. You need to be prepared, but only God can open a person's heart. Just keep directing them back to the specific words of the Bible.

Perhaps this is where we hop off the Isaiah train and thank him for his contribution to the argument? Not so fast. Paul quotes this very same Isaiah passage in Romans 14:6-12. Not surprisingly, he quotes it with the same point. Take your seat. We're not done yet.

Live and Die for Jesus
(Romans 14:1-14 & Isaiah 45:23)

Paul quotes Isaiah 45:23 twice. We just looked at the letter to the believers at Philippi (Phil 2:10-11), where the quote shows that Jesus is Yahweh. The second quote is in Paul's letter to the church in Rome, and it shows exactly the same thing.

In Romans 14:1-14, we're encouraged to make every decision and action based on the Lord Jesus. In this passage, notice how "Lord" and "God" are used interchangeably:

"Accept him whose faith is weak, without passing judgment on disputable matters. One man's faith allows him to eat everything, but another man, whose faith is weak, eats only vegetables. The man who eats everything must not look down on him who does not, and the man who does not eat everything must not condemn the man who does, for <u>God</u> has accepted him. Who are you to judge someone else's servant? To his own <u>master (lord)</u> he stands or falls. And he will stand, for the <u>Lord</u> is able to make him stand. … He who regards one day as special, does so to the <u>Lord</u>. He who eats meat, eats to the <u>Lord</u>, for he gives thanks to <u>God</u>; and he who abstains, does so to the <u>Lord</u> and gives thanks to <u>God</u>. For none of us lives to himself alone and none of us dies to himself alone. If we live, we live to the <u>Lord</u>; and if we die, we die to the <u>Lord</u>. So, whether we live or die, we belong to the <u>Lord</u>."
(Romans 14:1-8)

Now who exactly is this Lord and God? The next verse seals it:

"For this very reason, <u>Christ</u> died and returned to life so that <u>he might be the Lord</u> of both the dead and the living." *(14:9)*

Christ is the Lord of the living, meaning that He controls both the throttle and rudder. Who in the universe can claim such a thing? Verse 9 says that He is not only the Lord of the living, but since He rose from the dead, we know that He is the Lord of heaven and hell and everywhere in between. Since Christ is the "Lord of both the dead and the living," verse 10 concludes that He is therefore God and Judge:

> **"You, then, why do you judge your brother? Or why do you look down on your brother? For we will all stand before <u>God's</u> judgment seat."** *(14:10)*

When it comes down to it, each person is going to stand before Christ, because Christ is the Holy One, the One by whom all will be measured and judged. To prove who Christ is beyond any question, Paul then quotes Isaiah 45:23:

> **"It is written:**
> **"*'As surely as I live,' says the <u>Lord</u>,***
> ***'every knee will bow before me;***
> ***every tongue will confess to <u>God</u>.'* "** *(from Isaiah 45:23)*
> **So then, each of us will give an account of himself to <u>God</u>."**
> *(Romans 14:11-12)*

If you had any doubt that Lord and God were the same, Paul settles it by this quote from Isaiah. In Isaiah, Yahweh is speaking, and He is surely both Lord and God. In the verse just previous to the quote, Yahweh calls Himself the *only* God:

> **"...for I am God, and there is no other.**
> **By myself I have sworn,** ("as surely as I live")
> **my mouth has uttered in all integrity**
> **a word that will not be revoked:**
> **Before me every knee will bow;**
> **by me every tongue will swear."** *(Isaiah 45:22-23)*

You can't get around it. It's like an 18 wheeler jackknifed crosswise in the road. Paul is certain that Jesus is Lord and Jesus is God and Jesus is Yahweh.

To top it off, in Romans 14:14, Jesus is again stated to be the Lord:

"As one who is in the <u>Lord Jesus</u>, I am fully convinced that no food is unclean in itself." *(Romans 14:14)*

In what movies you support, whom you date, in the time you spend with your family, and in any gray area, Romans 14 says do it all to please Jesus. We're not living for ourselves, but for Him. He's the Master, and we will have to give account directly to Him someday. It says to move forward and take risks solely based on Him. It says to avoid some places and items based on knowledge of Him - Paul calls this "dying" to yourself (Romans 10:7). Every decision in life is based on Him, whether I support a gambling casino with the money He's entrusted to me, whether I copy my friend's homework, or whether I pay dues to a union that promotes what Christ condemns. I don't base my actions on emotions or on what I desire or what is convenient, because Jesus is the Lord of me. He is Yahweh.

Jesus is the Standard
(1 Peter 3:15 & Isaiah 8:12-13)

Ahaz was one of the most wicked kings that Jerusalem ever had. He didn't care at all about following the LORD and led the people of South Israel down the same path. But Ahaz had two deadly enemies aiming for him: North Israel, and the nearby country of Aram.

As Ahaz was in the palace, messengers came running, out of breath, and coughing the worst news. His two enemies had banded together and formed an alliance. They planned to do a final sweep of South Israel like a broom sweeps up dirt into a dust pan. Ahaz and all Jerusalem were sweating:

"Now the house of David (Ahaz) was told, 'Aram has allied itself with Ephraim' (North Israel); **so the hearts of Ahaz and his people were shaken, as the trees of the forest are shaken by the wind."**
(Isaiah 7:2) (Also see 2 Kings 16 and 2 Chronicles 28)

Aram and North Israel came against Jerusalem with a vengeance. However, they could not quite take Jerusalem's wall before they had to abandon the siege. Ahaz knew one thing, though: They would be back. With a following of military officers, government leaders, and concerned people, Ahaz went out through the massive city gates to the main water supply of the city. It was a small pond which had a man-made channel to the city. This was a weak spot. Since the pool was *outside* the city wall, an enemy could use it for himself. What was even worse was that the enemy could block the water from getting to the city. They might even poison it. Ahaz deliberated: *Hm...Maybe we could somehow block it up to prevent them from using it. If we cut a tunnel, maybe we could bring the water under the wall. Or if we had time, we could possibly build a new wider wall around it ...if we had time.*

It was at this place that the Lord told the prophet Isaiah to intercept Ahaz and the crowd with him:

> **"Then the LORD said to Isaiah, '…meet Ahaz at the end of the aqueduct of the Upper Pool, on the road to the Washerman's Field.' Say to him, 'Be careful, keep calm and don't be afraid. Do not lose heart because of these two smoldering stubs of firewood … Aram, Ephraim and Remaliah's son have plotted your ruin, saying, *'Let us invade Judah; let us tear it apart and divide it among ourselves, …'* Yet this is what the Sovereign LORD says, 'It will not take place, it will not happen' "**
>
> *(Isaiah 7:3-7)*

The LORD is saying, *Your enemies are making all kinds of plans, but this is what I say. I have resolved to protect Jerusalem. Now, put your trust in Me, not in politics or military or a wall or someone else to come rescue you. Then you will have no reason to fear them or anyone else. You'll be calm and at peace when all around you is danger and in turmoil and trouble.*

Ahaz frowned at Isaiah with scorn and brushed him away. Instead of listening to Isaiah, he drafted a letter and sent it with messengers to the king of Assyria. This was a last ditch plea. Assyria was a very wicked nation, but a sure powerful one:

> **"Ahaz sent messengers to say to Tiglath-Pileser king of Assyria, *'I am your servant and vassal. Come up and save me out of the hand of the king of Aram and of the king of Israel, who are attacking me.'* "**
>
> *(2 Kings 16:7)*

Along with the letter, he sent a trailer piled high with crates of gold and cash. He got some from the palace and some from his princes, but he also had sent a SWAT team into the LORD's temple to bag the people's offerings. Everyone agreed that Assyria was their only hope, *Only they have men and weapons enough to help. Anyone who*

*disagrees is, in fact, an enemy of this city. If you are against Assyria giving us aid, you are no patriot. You __want__ Jerusalem to be wiped off the map! Anyone who is against this is **conspiring** against us.* But the LORD warned Isaiah against following the majority:

"The LORD spoke to me with his strong hand upon me, warning me not to follow the way of this people. He said: 'Do not call conspiracy everything that these people call conspiracy; **do not fear what they fear, and do not dread it.** The LORD Almighty is the one you are to regard as holy, __he is the one__ you are to fear, __he is the one__ you are to dread' " *(Isaiah 8:11-13)*

Holy means, "the standard," or "set apart," or simply, "different." The LORD says to Isaiah, *No matter what anyone else does, whether they listen or not, YOU fear Me as the Holy One. Treat My words as the highest authority. Treat Me as set apart from the rest, let it be your goal to obey Me.* Fearing the LORD means obeying Him over anyone else, treating Him as master and boss. For Isaiah, fearing the LORD meant looking like a traitor. Isaiah stands firm, though:

"I will wait for the LORD, who is hiding his face from the house of Jacob. I will put my trust in him." *(Isaiah 8:17)*

Isaiah has dug in his heels. He's risking all. It looks like the LORD is hiding Himself and not coming through, but Isaiah is determined to obey, no matter what. This stubborn trust is exactly the kind of trust the LORD is looking for even to this very day. Fear of the LORD is why Isaiah was willing to be one man against the crowd, to confront the powerful, and to be called a traitor and every name in the book.

Now let's get to the point. Isaiah 8:12-13 says:

"Do not call conspiracy everything that these people call conspiracy **do not fear what they fear, and do not dread it. The LORD Almighty is the one you are to regard as holy**, he is the one you are to fear, he is the one you are to dread." *(Isaiah 8:12-13)*

Many centuries later, Peter quotes this very passage under the inspiration of God:

"But even if you should suffer for what is right, you are blessed. <u>Do not fear what they fear; do not be frightened. But in your hearts set apart Christ as Lord.</u> Always be prepared to give an answer to everyone who asks you to give the reason for the hope that you have."
(1 Peter 3:14-15)

The English wording somewhat obscures the fact that it's a direct quote. "Set apart" in 1 Peter 3:15 means *exactly* the same as "regard as holy" in Isaiah 8:12.

You will notice something very important with this quote. Do not miss it! In Isaiah 8:13, whom are we told to fear? The LORD. The capital letters, LORD, are the clue in your English version that this is the Hebrew name Yahweh. The Bible says from cover to cover that only He deserves fear. He is the Holy One.

Peter quotes Isaiah, but there's a major difference. Instead of setting the LORD as The Standard, Peter substitutes another. He says to not fear anyone as the standard except <u>Christ</u>. Treat Jesus as the ultimate authority. Regard Jesus as the Holy One. In all that you do, measure it up to Jesus exclusively as the very standard defining right and wrong. Whether you are at work, when you are alone or in a crowd, when you watch TV, when you spend your money, when you react to all kinds of situations around you, treat Jesus as the master.

How can Peter say this? We know that the LORD, the Creator Himself, demands that all follow Him <u>exclusively</u>. He alone is the Holy One. He alone is to be feared. No one else can even come close. All comes clear when you see that Jesus IS the LORD, Yahweh in the flesh. Peter certainly believed that. (No wonder why we concentrate so much on Jesus!)

If you are like Isaiah, and it seems like everyone and everything are against you, seek to obey Jesus. If you obey Him, more strength is with you than against you. Now, do not fool yourself... not obeying Him is not fearing Him, even if you say you do. Whether you are wasting time, gossiping, gambling, or dating an unbeliever, you're lying to yourself. You cannot have it both ways. Will you dedicate and set apart your life from this point onward to serve Jesus? In all that you do or do not do, will you measure it up to Him alone, *The Standard*?

All Your Eggs in One Basket
(Romans 10:9-13 & Joel 2:32)

When I (Peter) applied to college, I did a load of research and visited different colleges throughout New York. I studied the different options and spoke with a number of friends who had attended each of these. When the time came, I only applied to the one that I *really* wanted to attend. I put all my eggs in one basket. If I did not get in, life would look a lot different now.

The obvious risk was that I had nothing to fall back on. When you "put all your eggs in one basket," you are taking a high risk. You must have full confidence in your course of action before you make it.

Romans 10:9-13 is a stop on the famous "Romans Road." It's no wonder. I bet it says more than you realize:

"That if you confess with your mouth, *'Jesus is Lord,'* and believe in your heart that God raised him from the dead, you will be saved. For it is with your heart that you believe and are justified, and it is with your mouth that you confess and are saved. As the Scripture says, *'Anyone who trusts in him will never be put to shame.'* For there is no difference between Jew and Gentile — the same Lord is Lord of all and richly blesses all who call on him, for, *'Everyone who calls on the name of the Lord will be saved.'* "
(Romans 10:9-13)

Verse 9 says that the difference between your eternal life and the sound of the gavel pounding the eternal bench is putting all your eggs in the fact that "Jesus is Lord." Already we're wondering how in the world Jesus could have such authority. It doesn't fit that He is a mere earthly lord who has the authority over life and death and the eternal destiny of souls.

Verse 12 says there is one Lord. He is the Lord of both Jews and non-Jews, and will certainly answer when either cry out to Him. This One Lord was named as Jesus in verse 9.

Now it comes to a focal point in verse 13:

> **"for, 'Everyone who calls on the name of the <u>Lord</u> will be saved.' "**
> *(Romans 10:13)*

You'll understand the power of these words when seeing that Paul is quoting from the Old Testament prophet Joel. Joel said:

> **"And everyone who calls on the name of the LORD will be saved"**
> *(Joel 2:32)*

Joel is recording Yahweh's words, and the capital LORD in your Bible is the tip. Yahweh is saying anyone who calls to Him will be saved. If you read Joel, you will see that this passage is a prophecy of the days we live in, AD days, the last days. (For you Latin-challenged, AD is *Anno Domini*, the "year of our Lord.") Paul quotes this from Joel, which is certainly about calling to <u>Yahweh</u> for saving, but Paul is using it to authenticate and prove that anyone who calls on <u>Jesus</u> will be saved. The conclusion is obvious. You can see why we titled this book as we did.

Romans 10 is saying that being saved from the just consequence of sin is more than just spouting off the words, *"Jesus is Lord."* Don't think that you're saved because of some words you simply repeated when you were a kid. This passage is saying you must confess (the word means to agree to the fact, to put all your eggs in one basket) that Jesus is Yahweh Himself. You must confess that Yahweh is the One who descended to earth, died, and rose from the dead. (By the way, this clarifies 1 Corinthians 12:3, *"...no one can say, 'Jesus is Lord,' except by the Holy Spirit."*)

Whether you're a Jew or not, the requirements for being saved are the same according to this passage. Don't be fooled into thinking that if you're a Jew you're automatically "in" (Romans 2:28).

Jesus is greater than any prophet or saint or Mary or Mohammed or any mere angel. He is the One who predates time. He raises up presidents and takes them out at will. He has the strength of the Almighty. He is the Commander of fighters. He is the Judge whose verdict cannot be reversed. His authority has a greater range, greater reach, greater extent, and greater magnitude than any mere created being. He is the King of Glory.

Complaining and gossip are not just against people. Lying is not against a mere custom. Pornography and gambling are not merely against state laws. These are all against the Greatest One, The Standard, Jesus Himself. Do you see the seriousness and the magnitude of the situation?

Sin is against the Greatest One to sin against, and therefore the price is the ultimate. None other than the Creator Himself could pay the price you owed. No angel. No saint. The Creator lowered Himself from the realms of glory, disgracing Himself, shaming Himself. This was to pay **your** price. If you have not put all your eggs in this basket and submitted your life to Jesus as LORD, this is the time.

Jesus Is No Angel
(Hebrews 1 & Psalm 102)

If you interviewed the regular guy on the street, he'd likely tell you that angels help you, listen to your prayers, can perform miracles, know the future, and have always lived. They're up near God's level.

This is dead wrong.

Angels are merely servants, messengers of the Eternal One. The Almighty speaks and they jump. They have not lived forever. They cannot be in two places at once. Their knowledge is limited. They are created beings, and there is an enormous, a vast, an immense, and in fact an infinite difference between any created being and The Creator.

The New Testament quotes Psalm 102 maybe in a surprising way (though, by now, hopefully not too surprising to you). Psalm 102 is addressed to Yahweh. Verses 1 and 12 make this clear:

> **"Hear my prayer, O LORD; let my cry for help come to you...**
> **But you, O LORD, sit enthroned forever..."** *(Psalm 102:1, 12)*

In English versions of the Old Testament, remember that the capital LORD tells us that this is the Hebrew name Yahweh. Now look down at verses 25-27:

> **"In the beginning you laid the foundations of the earth,**
> **and the heavens are the work of your hands.**
> **They will perish, but you remain;**
> **they will all wear out like a garment.**
> **...But you remain the same,**
> **and your years will never end."** *(Ps 102:25-27)*

The "you" is Yahweh, to whom the Psalm is addressed. Yahweh has gripped David's mouth, and David is writing inspired words to Yahweh, the only Creator, and the only One who is eternal.

Now turn to Hebrews. The point of the book of Hebrews is, "Jesus is superior." He is superior to the prophet Moses (3:1-6), superior to the great leader Joshua (4:8-9), superior to The Law (7:18), superior to the priests (7:23-8:6), and superior to the Old Testament sacrifices (9:11-10:18). The point of the first chapter of Hebrews is that Jesus is superior to angels. The author goes back and forth as he makes a sharp and clear-cut distinction between Jesus and angels.

He starts by setting the focus on Jesus…

"In the past God spoke to our forefathers through the prophets at many times and in various ways, but in these last days he has spoken to us by his Son, whom he appointed heir of all things, and through whom he made the universe. The Son is the radiance of God's glory and the exact representation of his being, sustaining all things by his powerful word. After he had provided purification for sins, he sat down at the right hand of the Majesty in heaven." *(Hebrews 1:1-3)*

Now he contrasts Jesus with the angels…

"So he became as much superior to the angels as the name he has inherited is superior to theirs. For to which of the angels did God ever say, *'You are my Son; today I have become your Father'*? Or again, *'I will be his Father, and he will be my Son'*"? *(vs. 4-5)*

Now back to Jesus…

"And again, when God brings his firstborn into the world, he says, *'Let all God's angels worship him.'*" *(vs. 6)*

Back to angels, who are only servants…

"In speaking of the angels he says, *'He makes his angels winds, his servants flames of fire.'*" *(vs. 7)*

But Jesus is God and King, the Master of the angels…

"But about the Son he says, *'Your throne, O God, will last for ever and ever, and righteousness will be the scepter of your kingdom. You have loved righteousness and hated wickedness; therefore God, your God, has set you above your companions by anointing you with the oil of joy.'* He also says, *'In the beginning, O Lord, you laid the foundations of the earth, and the heavens are the work of your hands. They will perish, but you remain; they will all wear out like a garment. You will roll them up like a robe; like a garment they will be changed. But you remain the same, and your years will never end.'* " *(vs. 8-12)*

You think angels are so high and powerful…

"To which of the angels did God ever say, *'Sit at my right hand until I make your enemies a footstool for your feet'* " ? *(vs. 13)*

Pay attention; angels are servants…

"Are not all angels ministering spirits sent to serve those who will inherit salvation? We must pay more careful attention, therefore, to what we have heard, so that we do not drift away. For if the message spoken by angels was binding, and every violation and disobedience received its just punishment, how shall we escape if we ignore such a great salvation? This salvation, which was first announced by the Lord, was confirmed to us by those who heard him." *(1:14-2:3)*

But Jesus is the ruler…

"It is not to angels that he has subjected the world to come, about which we are speaking…" *(2:5)*

Back and forth, the contrast is enhanced. Angels and Jesus are poles apart — there's a night and day difference.

Now we come to the main point. The ultimate contrast is when Hebrews 1:10-12 quotes from Psalm 102:25-27:

"He also says, (he's still talking about Jesus)
'In the beginning, O Lord, you laid the foundations of the earth,
and the heavens are the work of your hands.
They will perish, but you remain;
they will all wear out like a garment.
You will roll them up like a robe;
like a garment they will be changed.
But you remain the same,
and your years will never end.' " *(Hebrews 1:10-12)*

As we saw, Psalm 102 is addressed directly to Yahweh, the One Creator. At this point in Hebrews, it is talking about Jesus, and the words of Psalms 102 are applied directly to Jesus. It's saying that Jesus is the One who laid the foundations of the earth, Jesus is the Only Creator, Jesus is the Eternal One. There's no mistaking, Jesus is no angel! It's saying that Jesus is Yahweh.

Do you pray to a guardian angel? There are hundreds of prayers to Yahweh recorded in the Bible, by Abraham, David, Nehemiah, Isaiah, Daniel, Jonah, Moses, Hannah, Elijah, Hezekiah, and many others. But there is no example in the entire Bible of any prophet or king or Christian or anyone making a prayer to an angel. Stephen, though, was a godly man and filled with the Holy Spirit. He saw who Jesus was and prayed directly to Him at his time of greatest need (Acts 7:54-60). When your work is in jeopardy, when you're hurting for a friend, when your parent's health is declining, or when things are out of control, you can do the same.

Triumph March of the King
(Ephesians 4:7-8 & Psalm 68:18)

David wrote Psalm 68 as a praise song addressed to Yahweh:

"Sing to God, sing praise to his name,
...his name is the LORD" *(Psalm 68:4)*

A fitting title might be, *"Triumph March"* or *"Procession to the Palace."* In the Psalm, Yahweh trounces all opposition, and then He ascends with a huge procession (vs. 18, 24-27) to the temple in Jerusalem. The motorcade has seemingly endless row upon row of nobles and captives, bands cranking, singers, and flags waving. Yahweh is the King ascending to His palace (vs. 24). It's more than a palace, it's a holy place (vs. 24 and 35). You could call it a "palace-temple." The LORD dwells there (vs. 16, 18), so the palace-temple is truly the "abode of God."

David has in mind two things: The first is the special tent (tabernacle) that he set up in Jerusalem for the ark of the covenant:

"[David] and the entire house of Israel brought up the ark of the Lord with shouts and the sound of trumpets. ...They brought the ark of the Lord and set it in its place inside the tent that David had pitched for it." *(2 Samuel 6:12-17)*

Yet, David knows that the Creator is surely not confined to any man-made construction (Psalm 103:19)! The tabernacle, and later temple, was only a **copy** of the true one in heaven:

"...a sanctuary that is a copy and shadow of what is in heaven. This is why Moses was warned when he was about to build the

tabernacle: 'See to it that you make everything according to the pattern shown you on the mountain.'" *(Hebrews 8:5)*

"For Christ did not enter a man-made sanctuary that was only a copy of the true one; he entered heaven itself" *(Hebrews 9:24)*

Now, let's get to the point. Right in the middle of Psalm 68 we have a description of Yahweh ascending:

"When you ascended on high,
you led captives in your train;
you received gifts from men
...that you, O LORD God, might dwell there." *(Psalm 68:18)*

A thousand years later, God inspired Paul to quote Psalm 68:

"But to each one of us grace has been given as Christ apportioned it. This is why it says:
 'When he ascended on high,
 he led captives in his train
 and gave gifts to men.' " *(Ephesians 4:7-8)*

Psalm 68 is certainly addressing Yahweh Himself. Here, though, Paul quotes it and says that *Jesus is the One of Psalm 68*. Jesus descended from heaven, Jesus ascended back to heaven, Jesus is leading captives, Jesus is giving gifts. Then Paul goes on to list the gifts that Jesus apportioned:

"It was he who gave some to be apostles, some to be prophets, some to be evangelists, and some to be pastors and teachers"
(Eph 4:11)

Clearly, the New Testament is assuming that Jesus is Yahweh.

Let's address an off-topic issue you might have noticed. Why does Psalm 68 say that Yahweh **receives** gifts, while the quote in Ephesians 4 says Yahweh **gives** gifts?

It is possible that Paul is quoting from both verse 18 and verse 35, which tells of Yahweh **giving** gifts:

"The God of Israel is He who <u>gives</u> strength and power to His people." *(Psalm 68:35)*

An alternative is that maybe the intention of Yahweh receiving gifts was to then give them.

Whatever the answer, the point of this chapter is not affected.

Can You Hear Me Now?

Seeing Him As He Is
(John 12 & Isaiah 6)

We have a blindfold wrapped around our head but don't even realize it. In our mind we imagine a God near our level. We make Him out to be a doting grandfather in the sky. Tame. Meek. We think we can satisfy Him by going to church each week, maybe dropping something into the plate, or being a good person. But it is all in the mind. We think we see clearly, but it's dreamed up. We ignore that He is the Holy One. He is the standard of right and wrong, and we ignore how guilty we are in His sight. We ignore that He is the One who holds our very life in His hands.

Isaiah thought he saw clearly until the day when the blindfold was stripped off. Afterward, he was willing to go against the flow, to be seen as a traitor to his own countrymen, and to raise both government and respected religious leaders to a boil. It didn't matter what anyone else thought or did, he had seen Him and this changed everything. Isaiah wrote:

"In the year that King Uzziah died, I saw the Lord seated on a throne, high and exalted, and the train of his robe filled the temple. Above him were seraphs, each with six wings: With two wings they covered their faces, with two they covered their feet, and with two they were flying." *(Isaiah 6:1-2)*

The Hebrew word "seraph" means "to burn," so these are the "burning ones." They are some rank of angelic creature that appear as the brightness of an acetylene torch or of an electrical arc. Bright enough to make you dive for cover. You think they're frightening? These "burning ones" cover their faces like babies crying for their mothers in the presence of The Great One. They cover their feet in unworthiness in His presence. Isaiah tells what he saw:

"And they were calling to one another:
'Holy, holy, holy is the LORD Almighty;
the whole earth is full of his glory.' " *(Isaiah 6:3)*

They call and echo to each other, "Holy!" It means, "He is the standard." The meaning is that all must measure up to Him. It's sealed with triple strength.

"At the sound of their voices the doorposts and thresholds shook and the temple was filled with smoke. 'Woe to me!' I cried. 'I am ruined! For I am a man of unclean lips, and I live among a people of unclean lips, and *my eyes have seen the King, the LORD Almighty.'* " *(Isaiah 6:4-5)*

When they pronounce the Name, all heaven goes nuclear. The very foundations shudder. Detonation. It's worse than a volcanic eruption, the explosion of an atom bomb, the magnitude 10.0 earthquake.

Isaiah looks and screams in terror. His heart seizes. His eyes open wide in fear. His stomach jumps to his throat and he looks for a way to scramble, to dive for cover behind a rock or tree or whatever he could huddle behind. Not from the Burning Ones, but from the One that caused them to cover their faces. Nothing is sufficient to hide him from His view. Sweat pours down Isaiah's pale face. He feels shamed, exposed, and dirty to the core. The All-seeing One's vision penetrates right through him. All secrets are out.

Who did he see? What is His name? In Hebrew, יהוה. In English, **YHWH**. Some pronounce it Yahweh. Or Jehovah. This is the name He gave Himself to Moses at the burning bush. It's the name for the One who inscribed with His finger the ten commands on rock. In the Bible, this name is <u>never</u> applied to a man, or an angel, or to any creature. It is the unique name of the One and Only God. So great was the reverence of the Jews for the name that they would not even speak it. That's why even today, we do not know for certain how to pronounce it. When reading the Scriptures in the temple or synagogue, if a rabbi came to this name, he would substitute another word, like Adonai, which means, "master." This was a euphemism for The Name. We still use the all capital letters, LORD, euphemism in our English Bibles.

The Name means, "Being One." He is the only One in this universe who is uncreated. Isaiah saw Him. He exclaims:

"My eyes have seen the King, the LORD Almighty" *(Isaiah 6:5)*

The LORD tells him to go proclaim a sour message: **"Make the heart of this people calloused; make their ears dull and close their eyes. Otherwise they might see with their eyes, hear with their ears, understand with their hearts, and turn and be healed."** (Isaiah 6:10) Not an assignment you volunteer for. But Isaiah had seen Him, and this made all the difference. He obeyed.

Many years later, John quotes this very account that Isaiah had written:

"Even after Jesus had done all these miraculous signs in their presence (especially raising Lazarus, 11:47, 12:18)**, they still would not <u>believe in him</u>."** *(John 12:37)*

Believe in whom? The verses just previous (35 and 36) tell us. Jesus is the main character of these chapters, and believing in Him is the theme. John goes on:

"This was to fulfill the word of Isaiah the prophet: *'Lord, who has believed our message and to whom has the arm of the Lord been revealed?'*

For this reason they could not <u>believe</u>, because, as Isaiah says elsewhere: *'He has blinded their eyes and deadened their hearts, so they can neither see with their eyes, nor understand with their hearts, nor turn—and I would heal them.'*

Isaiah said this because he saw Jesus' glory and spoke about him.

Yet at the same time many even among the leaders <u>believed in him</u>. But because of the Pharisees they would not confess their

faith for fear they would be put out of the synagogue; for they loved praise from men more than praise from God."
(John 12:38-43)

The key sentence is verse 41. Literally, it says, "These things Isaiah said when he saw His glory and spoke of Him." Who is the "his" and "him"? John is talking about believing in Jesus. It's both at the beginning of the passage:

"Even after <u>Jesus</u> had done all these miraculous signs in their presence, they still would not <u>believe in him</u>." *(John 12:37)*

and after:

"Then Jesus cried out, *'When a man believes in me...'* "
(John 12:44)

The "him" is so obvious that many translators have substituted in the obvious name for the pronoun: Jesus.

It's clear who Isaiah saw. Isaiah saw Yahweh. But in John 12:41, John says Isaiah, in fact, saw Jesus. John believed that Jesus was the same as Yahweh.

What happens when you leave a guy alone, just him with his computer and his internet connection? His door is closed. He sits so that the monitor is facing away from the door. It's an odd time for anyone to come in anyway. There are no fences preventing him from going where he wants. What happens? If he is convinced that Jesus is Yahweh and has submitted his life to Him, he doesn't need a fence — in this case, in the form of company internet monitoring or the boss coming in periodically to check. He knows that he will face the Lord Jesus, none lower than Yahweh Himself, and will have to give account. He realizes the depth of the payment that was paid for him and wants to please Him no matter if there is a fence or not. What about you?

The Children Got It Right
(Matthew 21:16 & Psalm 8:2)

It's amazing to think that people have been singing this song before Columbus sailed the ocean blue, before Mohammed took Mecca, before the Great Wall of China was so great. And I sang it even last week in church. It was written in 1000 BC (that's 3000 years ago for you math experts). It's quoted by Paul, and Jesus Himself knew the lyrics by heart:

"O LORD, our Lord,
how majestic is your name in all the earth!
You have set your glory above the heavens." *(Psalm 8:1)*

The Psalm is addressed to capital LORD, which is the English clue that it's addressed to Yahweh. It begins, "Yahweh, our Lord…" The second word "Lord" is in lower case, which indicates that the Hebrew word is "Adonai." This means master or boss or owner. David is saying, *"Yahweh, No one else is our master as you are. Yahweh, your awesomeness is in full view of all."*

The second verse says that the One who designed and fabricated moon and stars and shipped them into position does not need some great orator to announce His greatness. The heavens themselves proclaim it. Ironically, Yahweh has decided to confound the "strong" who oppose Him by having mere little children praise Him:

"From the lips of children and infants you have ordained praise (or strength) because of your enemies, to silence the foe and the avenger." *(Psalm 8:2)*

Jesus probably sang this while chiseling and hauling and sweating in Nazareth. On the day we now call Palm Sunday, he quoted it by memory, but in a surprising way.

The air is tense in Jerusalem. The word is that today someone great is coming to town. The Roman authorities are on alert. The children can't keep their mind on math and Hebrew. The women are talking as they grind and milk. Then stuff starts happening:

> **"A very large crowd spread their cloaks on the road, while others cut branches from the trees and spread them on the road. The crowds that went ahead of him and those that followed shouted, *'Hosanna to the Son of David!' 'Blessed is he who comes in the name of the Lord!' 'Hosanna in the highest!'***
>
> **When Jesus entered Jerusalem, the whole city was stirred and asked, 'Who is this?' The crowds answered, 'This is Jesus, the prophet from Nazareth in Galilee.' ...The blind and the lame came to him at the temple, and he healed them. But when the chief priests and the teachers of the law saw the wonderful things he did and the children shouting in the temple area, *'Hosanna to the Son of David,'* they were indignant."** *(Matthew 21:8-15)*

Indignant means wicked mad (For you non-New Englanders, this means "extremely mad"). The ministers in Jerusalem are hot, ready to boil over. It is the kind of scene that would usually end in violence. It comes to a head when the children start echoing the cheer of their parents (vs. 9). The pastor of Jerusalem Baptist, the elders of Kidron Valley Pres, and the ministers of Torah Assembly of God disagree on various issues of theology — baptism, end time events, worship style — but they are all in agreement today. They're united:

> **"Do you hear what these children are saying?" they asked him.** *(Matt 21:15)*

Their twisted faces show their anger, "Do you hear what they're saying about <u>you</u>? Do you hear how they're praising you, like you were a god or something. Do you think nothing of the first commandment? Do you not

know the Scripture, "I will not yield my glory to another." *(Isaiah 48:11)* Who do you think you are? How dare you just accept this, consent to it, allow it!"

Jesus had indeed heard. But he did not stop the worship directed to him. The children were fulfilling the ancient prophecy. Ironically, they were the ones doing exactly what was right. Jesus' answer has no hint of wavering:

"Yes," replied Jesus, "have you never read,
'From the lips of children and infants you have ordained praise' **?"**
(Matt 21:16)

He quotes the ancient song of Psalm 8, the one foretelling children directly praising Yahweh Himself. Jesus is saying, *It is happening in front of your face.* The children ARE praising Yahweh (and in the presence of His enemies). It doesn't take too many brain cells to realize what Jesus is saying. Jesus is claiming to be Yahweh in the flesh.

To put all your money on this fact is certainly against the grain. It's even against what many so-called churches teach. You might be looked down upon as some sort of zealot or ignorant. Jesus' resurrection from the dead, though, proved that He is who He said He is. The biblical authors staked their reputations and lives on this fact. Therefore, you are in good company. We encourage you to press on and look for opportunities to draw others' attention to Jesus.

Summing up the "Top 10"

Jesus is the One True God, Yahweh who came down as a man. Paul believed it *(Phil 2 and Rom 14 vs. Isaiah 45:23; Eph 4:7-8 vs. Ps 68:18)*, John believed it *(Rev 4-5; Rev 22:13 vs. Is 44:6)*, Peter believed it *(1 Peter 3:15 vs. Isaiah 8:12)*, the author of Hebrews believed it *(Heb 1 vs. Ps 102)*, Jesus Himself claimed it clearly *(Jn 8 vs. Ex 3; Rev 22 vs. Isaiah 44:16; Mt 21:16 vs. Ps 8)*. Everything Yahweh is, Jesus is, but in flesh.

We have considered a number of specific passages. In the next chapter we will move from the trees to the forest.

5

God Down to the Core

Take a guess: What animal has thick, leathery, grey skin, has two ivory tusks, weighs more than a car, has four large toed feet, has large floppy ears, has a long trunk to grab and smell and trumpet and spray, eats vegetation, loves to eat peanuts, and has a short twisted tail?

You surely did not need this whole description to figure it out. The trunk and tusks would have settled it for certain. In the same way, who do you know that is able to create out of nothing, accepts worship by humans and angels, accepts prayer, is all-powerful, knows the future, and is present everywhere? You surely did not need this whole description to know that the answer is only Yahweh Himself.

Is Jesus 100% God, the Only True God, Yahweh Himself? Consider the evidence: The Bible says Jesus:

- **Existed before the creation of the world**
- **Created everything in the universe out of nothing**
- **Holds the laws of nature to this very hour**
- **Is unchanging**

- Is the first and the last, the A to Z
- Is present in multiple places at once
- Knows the future
- Is the very standard of right and wrong
- Has the authority to forgive a man's sin
- Has the authority to give eternal life
- Is rightly prayed to
- Is worshipped by all angels & will be by all creation
- His words are equal in authority to God's words
- All in the universe will bow and submit to Him as master
- Is the Judge on the final Day of Judgment
- His rule is eternal
- Has the same names as God
- Has the same attributes as God
- Does things that only God can do
- Makes the same claims as God
- Is given the same worship as is proper to God only
- Told people that knowing Him is the same as knowing God
- Told people that seeing Him is the same as seeing God
- Believing in Him is the same as believing in God
- Receiving Him is the same as receiving God

The pile of evidence is massive. It cannot be ignored. Since Jesus has the same set of "God-only" attributes, we can be certain that He is God (See the Appendix for the references). A similar case can be made that the Holy Spirit is 100% God, the Only True God, but that's for another day.

The Extreme Hijacker?

Have you ever noticed that Jesus seems to take over, to hijack, the New Testament? Look at these exclusively "God-things" he constantly claims:

"I know your deeds ... I am he who searches hearts and minds ... I am the resurrection and the life ... I am sending you prophets and wise men and teachers ... I am with you always ... *I will give you the crown of life* ... I am about to spit you out of my mouth ... <u>Then I will tell them plainly, 'I never knew you. Away from me, you evildoers!'</u> ... **Come to me, all you who are weary and burdened, and I will give you rest** ... Destroy this temple, and I will raise it again in three days ... I will raise him up at the last day ... To him who overcomes, I will give the right to eat from the tree of life ... My words will never pass away"

This takeover is right to the end of the Bible. The book of Revelation starts, *"The revelation of Jesus...,"* ends with Him, and He's the main focus all in between. The last chapter says that Jesus is coming soon, that Jesus gives the rewards, that Jesus sends the angel, that Jesus is the root and offspring of David, and gives the final blessing pronouncing, "the grace of the Lord Jesus." Jesus is even called the Word of God, the same name as is applied to the Bible itself.

Jesus has not hijacked the Word of God. Jesus rightly owns it. Feel free to offer an opposing viewpoint. The fact is simple: we are presenting a case that considers the major passages. We have not offered a few obscure passages to prove the point.

You no doubt have a few lingering questions. Let's see if these can be settled in the next chapter.

6

Answers to Common Objections

Before we go any further, let's answer some questions you might have. By now, this first one should be swirling around in your head. This is so important to understand that we probably should have put it in Chapter One.

Q1. Why is Jesus called the <u>Son of God</u> if he IS God?

Jesus is often called "Son of God." For example, the famous John 3:16 says,

"For God so loved the world that he gave his one and only <u>Son</u>, that whoever believes in him shall not perish but have eternal life." *(John 3:16)*

Here's the problem. Today, "Son of God" does not convey the *intended* meaning of the phrase. Therefore, it's not a good term to accurately describe Jesus to most people. If you tell someone that Jesus is the "Son of God," he will think that Jesus is less than God. We view a son lower than the father - either in strength, authority, height, intelligence, or age. The person might picture a weak little baby in a manger. This is the wrong understanding of the term.

We care about what the *biblical author* meant and what the *original readers* of the Bible understood by this term. To them, "Son of God" was an idiom (a figure of speech) which meant that Jesus is of the same essence and nature as God. It means that Jesus is God right down to the core. It means that He is made of the same "stuff" as God. For example, the son of a horse is a horse, having the same essence and nature of a horse. The son of a human is human, having the same essence and nature as a human. The son of God is God, having the same essence and nature as God. Since there is only *one* God and since Jesus claimed to be the *only* Son of God, Jesus is claiming to be fully God Himself.

Synonyms for "Son of God" are **"God incarnate"** (which means "God in the flesh") or **"God come down in human form."**

When Jesus claimed to be the "Son of God" and called God His father, the Jews understood that Jesus was claiming to be of the same nature and essence as God Himself, to be God in the flesh, and therefore was claiming to be God Himself. This was blasphemy and was why they tried to kill Him (per Leviticus 24:16):

"Jesus said to them, *'My Father is always at his work to this very day, and I, too, am working.'* For this reason the Jews tried all the harder to kill him; not only was he breaking the Sabbath, but he was even calling God his own Father, making himself equal with God." *(John 5:17-18)*

Jesus knew what they thought, but notice that He did not deny it. They heard exactly what He intended for them to hear.

Let's now move to Jesus' trial. During it, the high priest asked Jesus if He was the Son of God (which, from this passage, you can see is a synonym for "Christ."):

"The high priest said to him, 'I charge you under oath by the living God: Tell us if you are the Christ, the Son of God.' 'Yes, it is as you say,' Jesus replied. 'But I say to all of you: In the future you will see the Son of Man sitting at the right hand of the Mighty One and coming on the clouds of heaven.' " *(Matthew 26:63-64)*

Why did the high priest ask if Jesus were the Son of God rather than just ask if He were God? He could have, but he is being more specific in asking if Jesus is claiming to be "God incarnate." The high priest is asking if Jesus is claiming to be THE God, come down to earth. When Jesus admitted to being the Son of God, look at the violent reaction:

"Then the high priest tore his clothes and said, *'He has spoken blasphemy! Why do we need any more witnesses? Look, now you have heard the blasphemy. What do you think?'* 'He is worthy of death,' they answered. Then they spit in his face and struck him with their fists. Others slapped him and said, 'Prophesy to us, Christ. Who hit you?' " *(Matt 26:65-68)*.

What provoked such an explosive, intense response by the high priest and the Jews? There was accusation of blasphemy, ripping of clothes, spitting, striking, mocking, wanting to kill Him. They obviously understood that claiming to be Son of God was claiming to be someone much greater than a mere angel or prophet or some kind of spirit being. He was claiming to be THE God, God in human form, God incarnate,

Yahweh. Jesus had the opportunity to correct any misunderstanding, but He did not.

When Jesus was facing governor Pilate, do you know what the Jews' main charge against Him was? He claimed to be the Son of God:

"As soon as the chief priests and their officials saw him, they shouted, 'Crucify! Crucify!' But Pilate answered, 'You take him and crucify him. As for me, I find no basis for a charge against him.' The Jews insisted, 'We have a law, and <u>according to that law he must die because he claimed to be the Son of God.</u>' When Pilate heard this, he was even more afraid" *(John 19:6-8)*

This would be no big deal if He were only claiming to be an angel or spirit being or prophet. You don't kill people for claiming that. There is no law against claiming to be an angel, although you would probably consider him crazy. The Jews wanted to kill Jesus because He was claiming not to be someone inferior to God but claiming to be God Himself:

When Jesus defied natural laws by walking on water and then stopping a wild storm by His very voice, the disciples realized they had witnessed something that only THE Creator, THE God can do. They then call Him the Son of God. They are calling Him equal in nature to God, God incarnate:

"And when they climbed into the boat, the wind died down. Then those who were in the boat worshiped him, saying, '<u>Truly you are the Son of God.</u>' " *(Matt 14:32-33)*

Similarly, when the centurion saw nature quaking, he called Jesus the Son of God:

"When the centurion and those with him who were guarding Jesus saw the earthquake and all that had happened, they were terrified, and exclaimed, 'Surely he was the Son of God!' " *(Matt 27:54)*

When Nathanael realized that Jesus had seen him even when Jesus was not present, he realized that this was something only God Himself could do, and he immediately called Jesus the Son of God:

"How do you know me?" Nathanael asked. Jesus answered, "I saw you while you were still under the fig tree before Philip called you." Then Nathanael declared, "Rabbi, you are the Son of God; you are the King of Israel." Jesus said, "You believe because I told you I saw you under the fig tree. You shall see greater things than that." *(John 1:48-50)*

Even in the Old Testament, we see this understanding. When pagan king Nebuchadnezzar saw the miracle of the men walking in the fire, he concluded that the fourth man was an incarnate God. Even though this pagan believed in many gods, he still used the term to mean "god incarnate":

"He said, 'Look! I see four men walking around in the fire, unbound and unharmed, and the fourth looks like a son of the gods.' " *(Daniel 3:25)*

Satan came to Jesus and sarcastically said, "If you are the Son of God...":

"The tempter came to him and said, 'If you are the Son of God, tell these stones to become bread.' ...Then the devil took him to the holy city and had him stand on the highest point of the temple. 'If you are the Son of God,' he said, 'throw yourself down. ...' Jesus answered him, 'It is also written: 'Do not put the Lord your God to the test.' " *(Matt 4:3-7)*

Why doesn't Satan say, "If you are God?" He could have, but it was more specific for him to say, "If you are God incarnate." That is what Jesus was during the time when He was on earth. Jesus had humbled Himself to become a man (Phil 2:5-11).

Here is more evidence that, to the original readers, the "son of" phrase could mean being equal with the person or having the same nature or essence as that person.

In the following two passages, "sons of the prophets" is not talking about children of the prophets. It means, "the same nature as a prophet," which are in fact the prophets themselves:

"By the word of the LORD one of the <u>sons of the prophets</u> said to his companion, 'Strike me with your weapon,' but the man refused." *(1 Kings 20:35)*

"And Elisha came again to Gilgal: and there was a dearth (famine) in the land; and the <u>sons of the prophets</u> were sitting before him." *(2 Kings 4:38, KJV)* (Many translations have, "company of the prophets," but literally it is, "sons of the prophets")

In the following, is the Lord only observing children? No. "Sons of men" means the same as "men:"

"The LORD is in his holy temple; the LORD is on his heavenly throne. He observes the <u>sons of men</u>; his eyes examine them."
(Psalm 11:4)

"I, even I, am he who comforts you. Who are you that you fear <u>mortal men, the sons of men</u>, who are but grass, that you forget the LORD your Maker" *(Isaiah 51:12-13)*

"Sons of a sorceress" means having the nature of a sorceress:

"But you — come here, you <u>sons of a sorceress</u>, you offspring of adulterers and prostitutes!" *(Isaiah 57:3)*

"Sons of Thunder" means having a thunderous or violent nature:

"James son of Zebedee and his brother John (to them he gave the name Boanerges, which means <u>Sons of Thunder</u>)" *(Mark 3:17)*

Here, Jesus says "your sons" to mean "your people" or "other Jews:"

"And if I cast out demons by Beelzebub, by whom do <u>your sons</u> cast them out? Therefore they will be your judges."

(Luke 11:19, NKJV)

Some translations write, "followers," but the Greek word is "sons." "People" or "followers" would be valid interpretations, since Jesus is certainly not talking about children.

What does this all mean?

The title, "Son of God," means that Jesus is fully God, 100% God come down in the flesh. It is important to realize that Jesus claimed to be the <u>only one</u> having the same nature and essence as God, the only one who is both man and God (John 3:16,18).

If Jesus is the Son of God, He is of the same nature and essence as God Himself. He cannot be separated from God. He has the same authority, same strength, and same character as God. He is uncreated, the Ultimate Judge, the King. There was never a time when He didn't exist. However great you think Jesus is, He's greater. No wonder why we concentrate so much on Jesus!

Q2. If Jesus prayed to God, how could he BE God?

Jesus' main purpose in coming to earth was to die on the cross as a payment for sins (John 1:29). In order to do this, He took on a real flesh, blood, and bones body (Hebrews 4:15). Consider how incredible a limitation this was for the Creator Himself! Jesus willingly did it. Therefore, during the time He was on earth, He subjected Himself to the limitation to have to pray like the rest of us.

His taking on a body does not diminish the fact that He is Yahweh, but shows the depth of humility to which He was willing to lower Himself both to be our example and to secure our rescue from judgment.

During God's "visitation," God was in two places at one time, both on earth and in heaven. This should not be surprising. Is God not able to be in two places at once? When Yahweh walked with Adam in the garden (Gen 3:8), made the promise to Abram (Gen 12:7), and spoke face to face with Jacob before Jacob faced his brother Esau (Gen 32:30) was Yahweh not at the same time in any other place in the universe?

Q3. Isn't the word Trinity never in the Bible?

The word "Trinity" is not in the Bible, but neither is "omniscient," "independent," "omnipresent" and some other words we use to describe God. We use the word "Trinity" for the Bible's description of God's "three-ness." Right away, it must be pointed out that there are not three Gods. The Bible teaches from front to back that there is only One True God, but the Bible also teaches from front to back that He exists as a "three-ness." This characteristic of God's nature is unlike any other person.

The Bible teaches that God the Father, God the Son, and God the Holy Spirit are the <u>One</u> True God, but are still <u>distinct</u>. For example, God the Father did not die on the cross, which shows the distinction between the Father and the Son. Often someone will err on one side or the other: erring that Jesus is not the One True God, or erring that Jesus is not distinct from God the Father and the Holy Spirit and rejecting the Bible's teaching of the "three-ness."

It is important to recognize that Jesus did not give up any of His "God-ness" when He came to earth. He remained fully God, while taking on a human body. He chose to usually hold back His power while on earth. There is a big difference, though, between someone hacking off your arm and your willingly holding your arm behind your back.

To explain the Trinity, some explain that just like an egg has a shell, white, and yoke, God has three parts. This is inaccurate, because the shell is only a *part* of the egg and not *fully* egg. Jesus is not a part of God. Some have tried using water, saying that liquid, vapor, and ice are 3 forms of water. The problem is that the Father, Son, and Holy Spirit are not *forms* of God, each is fully God. Another illustration is flour, salt, and sugar mixed together in a batter. Once they're mixed, they're inseparable, which is good. The problem is that they are now not distinct. The Bible calls Jesus the radiance of God's glory (Heb 1:3). The radiance of the sun cannot be separated from the rest of the sun, but both are still distinct. All physical analogies break down; however, when it comes to this particular nature of God. The following old drawing tries to explain what the Bible teaches:

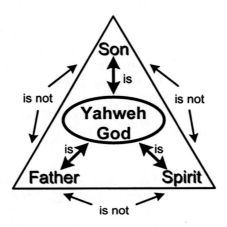

It is not essential to understand every detail of this nature of God that we call the Trinity. Much of it is described in the Bible, but there are still aspects about God that mere humans cannot understand. It is essential to understand, though, that Jesus is fully God. It will help your understanding to ask, "Can God be in two places at once?" Not half and half, but fully at once? We know this is true (Psalm 139). So, He could take on a human body and come to earth and be in heaven at the same time.

Q4. If Jesus is "firstborn," how can he be Yahweh?

If Jesus is the "firstborn," doesn't this imply that he is not the One True God? Here is the passage in consideration:

"He is the image of the invisible God, the <u>firstborn over all creation</u>. For by him all things were created: things in heaven and on earth, visible and invisible, whether thrones or powers or rulers or authorities; all things were created by him and for him. He is before all things, and in him all things hold together. And he is the head of the body, the church; he is the beginning and the firstborn from among the dead, so that in everything he might have the supremacy. For God was pleased to have all his fullness dwell in him" *(Colossians 1:15-19)*

You need to understand that "firstborn" can mean two things. It can mean the "first one born in a family." This is obvious:

"By faith (Moses) he kept the Passover and the sprinkling of blood, so that the destroyer of the firstborn would not touch the <u>firstborn</u> of Israel" (Hebrews 11:28)
"She gave birth to her <u>firstborn</u>, a son..." *(Luke 2:7)*

It can also mean "preeminent, greatest, or unsurpassed." Three examples:

- <u>Ephraim.</u>
  "They will come with weeping; they will pray as I bring them back. I will lead them beside streams of water on a level path where they will not stumble, because I am Israel's father, and Ephraim is my <u>firstborn</u> son." *(Jeremiah 31:9)*

  Ephraim was born <u>after</u> his brother Manassah, and yet is called the firstborn. Actually, here Ephraim is a synonym for the ten Northern tribes. So no matter how you look at it, it's not talking about the kid being the first out of the womb. The meaning is being preeminent.

- **David.**
  "I have exalted a young man from among the people. I have found David my servant; with my sacred oil I have anointed him. ...I will also appoint him my <u>firstborn</u>, the most exalted of the kings of the earth." *(Psalm 89:19-27)*

  Of Jesse's sons, Eliab was the oldest. Then came Abinadab and Shammah and five other brothers. David was the runt (1 Sam 16:6-11). In this case, being called firstborn had nothing to do with birth, but meant having a special relationship with God or a relationship of privilege. David is not first in time, but is first in privilege. The meaning of the word "firstborn" is influenced by the Old Testament custom of the birthright. In those times, the oldest son had the position of privilege. Here, God is going against the grain and giving that to David.

- **Israel.**
  "Then say to Pharaoh, 'This is what the LORD says: Israel is my <u>firstborn</u> son.' " *(Exodus 4:22)*

  Here, firstborn is obviously not used to mean first-created or first-birthed. The LORD is talking about a nation, not an individual.

So which option are we going to go with? This very passage in Colossians will help. In Colossians 1:18, Jesus is called "firstborn from among the dead," so this usage of firstborn nails down that firstborn does <u>not</u> mean "first-created" or "first-birthed." The next phrase clarifies what firstborn does mean, "so that in everything he might have the supremacy." See that the term "firstborn over all creation" further describes "image of the invisible God" and <u>distances Jesus from creation</u> rather than includes Him within it. Verse 15 is saying, *"Jesus is supreme, for He is the Creator of everything that has been created — let me spell this out for you — both invisible stuff and visible, physical and spiritual."*

Q5. Didn't Jesus say, "The Father is greater than I"?

Jesus said to His disciples:

"You heard me say, 'I am going away and I am coming back to you.' If you loved me, you would be glad that I am going to the Father, for the Father is greater than I." *(John 14:28)*

Remember that Jesus said this while He was on earth — during the time when He willingly lowered Himself and confined Himself to a regular human body. He did not say John 14:28 from the vantage point of heaven. See also Philippians 2:6-11.

Notice that in the book of Revelation, you don't see any submission. You don't see Jesus worshipping God. In fact, the attention of all of heaven is on Jesus.

Q6. Why did Jesus submit to the Father if he was really God?

When Jesus came to earth, He chose to take on a human body and limitations associated with that. Included in the limitations was that He chose to submit Himself to the Father. For example, the night before the cross, Jesus said:

> **"Father, if you are willing, take this cup from me; yet not my will, but yours be done."** *(Luke 22:42-43)*

Jesus willingly gave up the right to freely use His "God-only attributes," such as all-knowing, all-power, and all-presence. If He used these as before (John 1:3, 6:62, 17:5), He wouldn't be human! You can't be a human and yet be everywhere at the same time. You can't be a human and yet exist outside of time and see both the past and future like they were the continuous present. You can't be a human and have an utterly complete & unlimited knowledge of every microbe from sea to shining sea. Jesus chose to become a *human,* and therefore chose to limit Himself by using His "God-only attributes" only at the will of the Father. Jesus stressed that He *only* did the Father's will (Lk 22:42, Jn 6:38) and *always* did the Father's will (Jn 5:19, Jn 8:28). There could be no other option, since God cannot contradict Himself.

Why did the Creator of all things and the Mastermind of universal history humble Himself down so low as to become a human? **(1)** To be our example, and **(2)** to be a fitting substitute for us when He paid the terrible and awesome price on the cross. His love is the root of it.

Realize that just because Jesus submitted Himself to the Father, it does not necessarily mean that He is any less than the Father. When I submit myself to my wife for a particular time or wish, it does not mean that I am any less human than she is.

Q7. *"The Son Himself Will Be Made Subject..."* ?

After salvation is completed, Paul says:

"When he has done this, then the Son himself will be made subject to him who put everything under him, so that God may be all in all." *(1 Corinthians 15:28)*

This verse is indeed obscure and difficult to understand. The exact phrase "all in all" is not used anywhere else in the Bible. This passage must be understood in light of the many passages very clearly teaching that Jesus has an **eternal** and **unending** kingdom and rule. These cannot be ignored:

"For to us a child is born, ...And he will be called ...**Everlasting Father ... Of the increase of his government and peace there will be no end.**" *(Isaiah 9:6-7)*

"He was given authority, glory and sovereign power; all peoples, nations and men of every language worshiped him. His dominion is an **everlasting dominion that will not pass away, and his kingdom is one that will never be destroyed.**" *(Daniel 7:14)*

"You will be with child and give birth to a son, and you are to give him the name Jesus. ...**he will reign over the house of Jacob forever; his kingdom will never end.**" *(Luke 1:31-33)*

"But about the Son he says, '**Your throne, O God, will last for ever and ever.**' " *(Hebrews 1:8)*

"You will receive a rich welcome into the **eternal kingdom of our Lord and Savior Jesus Christ.**" *(2 Peter 1:11)*

"The kingdom of the world has become the kingdom of our Lord and of his Christ, and **he will reign for ever and ever.**" *(Revelation 11:15)*
(See also Hebrews 5:6 and Revelation 22:3.)

Neither can we ignore the vast evidence that Jesus is the Lord of Glory, Final Judge, Uncreated One, and Yahweh Himself. We have also shown that the phrase "Son of God" means, *"God Himself in the flesh."* (See Q1.) Jesus took on a body for a time to accomplish the mission of paying the terrible price for people's offenses. 1 Corinthians 15:28 could be saying that when the mission is complete, the kingdom of Jesus will merge back with the kingdom of God the Father, as it was before He took on a body. Whatever the interpretation, it would be wrong to use this obscure passage to contradict the many clear passages just mentioned that say that Jesus will eternally be the King.

7

Conclusion: Go with the Evidence!

Rule #1 in Bible study is to *go with the majority.* Yes, we like to cheer for the underdog in politics or football, and we are quite satisfied to see the underdog win. When it comes to the Bible, though, you should never root for the underdog. In other words, it is foolish to base your beliefs on one or two obscure verses while ignoring the majority.

Rule #2 in Bible study is that you always *interpret the unclear using the clear.* In other words, go with the most obvious interpretation.

These two rules are essential and fundamental, like a rock solid foundation, because we know that God wants us to understand His word, even more than we want to understand it. That is why he wrote it:

"**Hear**, O heavens! **Listen**, O earth!
      For the LORD has spoken…" *(Isaiah 1:2)*

"**Come near, you nations, and listen;**
      pay attention, you peoples!" *(Isaiah 34:1)*

"**If my people would but listen to me,**
      if Israel would follow my ways…" *(Psalm 81:13)*

"If they do not <u>listen</u> to Moses and the Prophets, they will not be convinced even if someone rises from the dead." (Luke 16:31)

"Therefore I want you to know that God's salvation has been sent to the Gentiles, and they will <u>listen</u>!" (Acts 28:28)

Here's an example that we've all experienced to help clarify. Let's say my car is making a funny noise. I take it to a mechanic who tells me that I am on the verge of real trouble. If I do not get it fixed immediately, I am in for an expensive problem. Let's say I have all kinds of free time to get a second, third, fourth, and fifth opinion. I visit 50 mechanics! 49 of them say the same thing. I am on the cusp of show-stopping trouble. But, the 50th mechanic says that I could either be on the verge of trouble or it could just be nothing. What would you think of me if I said, *"Well, he said it could be nothing"* and I then continue down the road without having it fixed. You would probably think I was a dope. You would be right.

You might be able to find some verse that could be interpreted some other way. But are you going to take a verse that is somewhat fuzzy and use it to be the foundation of what you believe, to negate all the others? Or are you going to go with the mountain of clear evidence? More is at stake here than breaking down on the side of the highway.

What does all this evidence mean? If Jesus is Yahweh, He has a claim on your life. Knowing Him and serving Him is everything. Look what Jesus Himself did for you: He came down from heaven, humiliating Himself by taking on the body of a mere man, and was shamed and paid the heavy price you owed for your sin. If He Himself paid the price, consider how weighty the price is that you must owe. Jesus rose from the dead and was seen by over 500 witnesses, proving He's the real deal (1 Corinthians 15:1-11). Today, He offers to save you from Judgment Day and the condemning that you deserve in eternity. You have sinned against the Greatest One to sin against, but He is offering forgiveness and an arms-open welcome into His heaven. If you do not accept His payment, you will have to pay the price yourself. And you do not have payment enough.

Our culture is full of absentee parents. They rarely talk to their children and are distant from their children. God, however, is not like that. He is not content to be distant. He became a human so that He could show us His full character and be a real example for us. We never have to wonder what God is like or what He desires.

If you now realize that Jesus is the One you will face and are convinced of your guilt in His sight, you can accept His gift by crying out directly to Him in prayer, placing your trust in what He did for you on the cross, and submitting to Him as master:

"Lord Jesus, now I realize that you are Creator and Judge and God Himself. I am so sorry for treating myself as #1 and not caring about your will. I realize that I am guilty in your sight and heading for punishment in eternity. Though I do not deserve it, I need your forgiveness. I ask you to grant me the gift of eternal life. Thank you for saving me by dying for me on the cross. I want to live for you from now on. You said, 'Everyone who calls on the name of the Lord will be saved.' That includes me and I thank you."

These words aren't a magic formula to get to heaven. They are only meaningful if your heart is fully in agreement. Jesus knows the truth of the heart (Rev 2:23).

Are you in need? Not sure where you fit in this life? Not sure what decision to make? Stephen, a man "full of the Holy Spirit," prayed directly to Jesus at his most critical need:

> **"But Stephen, full of the Holy Spirit... While they were stoning him, Stephen prayed, 'Lord Jesus, receive my spirit.' Then he fell on his knees and cried out, 'Lord, do not hold this sin against them.' When he had said this, he fell asleep."** *(Acts 7:55, 59-60)*

Stephen prayed to Jesus because Jesus is no mere created being. If He were, He would not have been worthy or able to remove the sins of a single person, much less everyone throughout all time who has looked to Him in trust. You can submit your requests and cares to Jesus as Stephen did, because Jesus is Yahweh, and He cares for you.

Phil 2:6
Col 1:18

Appendix

The Full Case

The next few pages show the big picture, in outline form, where the Bible says that Jesus has the same names as God, has the same attributes as God, does things that only God can do, makes the same claims as God, and is given the same worship as is proper to God only. It is not exhaustive, but will give you a sense of the magnitude of the evidence:

1. Jesus existed before he chose to be born on earth:

Jesus was with the Father before the world began:
John 8:58-59 "'I tell you the truth,' Jesus answered, 'before Abraham was born, I am!'
John 17:5 "Father, glorify me in your presence with the glory I had with you before the world began."
Jesus came into the world, and came down from heaven:
John 3:13 "No one has ever gone into heaven except the one who came from heaven — the Son of Man."
John 16:28 "I came from the Father and entered the world; now I am leaving the world and going back to the Father." Also see John 3:31.

2. Jesus has the same names and titles as God:

Jesus is Mighty God & Everlasting Father:

Isaiah 9:6 "For to us a child is born... and the government will be on his shoulders. And he will be called ... Mighty God, Everlasting Father"

Jesus is Yahweh (Capital "LORD" is Yahweh or Jehovah):

John 8:58-59 "'I tell you the truth,' Jesus answered, 'before Abraham was born, I am!' At this, they picked up stones to stone him." Jesus called himself "I am", which is the same as Yahweh (see Exodus 3:14-15). See also use of "I am" in John 8:24 and 8:28.

Psalm 102:1,25 "Hear my prayer, O LORD ... in the beginning you laid the foundations of the earth, and the heavens are the work of your hands ... but you remain the same, and your years will never end." This is addressed to Yahweh, but Hebrews 1:10-12 applies this to Jesus, "In the beginning, O Lord, you laid the foundations of the earth..."

Philippians 2:10-11 "at the name of Jesus every knee should bow, in heaven and on earth and under the earth, and every tongue confess that Jesus Christ is Lord, to the glory of God the Father." This is a quote by Yahweh in Isaiah 45:23, "Before me every knee will bow; by me every tongue will swear."

Romans 14:6-12 "He who regards one day as special, does so to the Lord. He who eats meat, eats to the Lord, for he gives thanks to God; and he who abstains, does so to the Lord and gives thanks to God. ...If we live, we live to the Lord; and if we die, we die to the Lord. So, whether we live or die, we belong to the Lord. For this very reason, Christ died and returned to life so that he might be the Lord of both the dead and the living. You, then, why do you judge your brother? Or why do you look down on your brother? For we will all stand before God's judgment seat. It is written: "'As surely as I live,' says the Lord, 'every knee will bow before me; every tongue will confess to God.'" (quoted from Isaiah 45:23) So then, each of us will give an account of himself to <u>God</u>." The quote shows that Jesus is both Yahweh and God.

1 Peter 3:14-15 "Do not fear what they fear; do not be frightened. But in your hearts set apart Christ as Lord." This quotes Isaiah 8:12-13 "Do not call conspiracy everything that these people call conspiracy; do not fear what they fear, and do not dread it. The LORD Almighty is the one you are to regard as holy (set apart), he is the one you are to fear" *Note: "regard as holy" means "set apart."*

John 12:41 "These things Isaiah said when he saw His glory and spoke of Him." Compare Isaiah 6:3-8 with John 12:37-42. John says that Isaiah saw Jesus and Jesus is Yahweh.

Joel 2:32 "And everyone who calls on the name of the LORD will be saved" Acts 2:17-21 applies this quote to Jesus, "this is what was spoken by the prophet Joel: *'In the last days,... And everyone who calls on the name of the Lord will be saved.'"* Romans 10:9-13 also applies this quote to Jesus, "if you confess with your mouth, "Jesus is Lord,"... for, *'everyone who calls on the name of the Lord will be saved.'"*

Isaiah 40:3 "A voice of one calling: 'In the desert prepare the way for the LORD...'" This is a prophecy that John the Baptist would announce the coming of Yahweh. See also Matthew 3:1-3.

Psalm 27:1 "The LORD (Yahweh) is my light and my salvation - whom shall I fear?" Jesus made this same claim, "I am the light of the world. Whoever follows me will never walk in darkness, but will have the light of life." (John 8:12)

Jeremiah 23:5-6 "The days are coming," declares the LORD, "when I will raise up to David a righteous Branch, a King who will reign wisely and do what is just and right in the land. ...This is the name by which he will be called: Yahweh Our Righteousness."

Psalm 23:1 "The LORD (Yahweh) is my Shepherd." Jesus applied this to himself, "I am the good shepherd." (John 10:11,14, Hebrews 13:20, 1 Peter 5:4, Rev 7:17.)

Psalm 68:18-19 "When you ascended on high, you led captives in your train; you received gifts from men ...that you, O LORD God, might dwell there." Ephesians 4:7-8 quotes this with the point of saying it refers to Jesus.

Jesus is God:

John 1:1 "In the beginning was the Word, and the Word was with God, and the Word was God."

John 5:17-18 "Jesus said to them, 'My Father is always at his work to this very day, and I, too, am working.' For this reason the Jews tried all the harder to kill him; not only was he breaking the Sabbath, but he was even calling God his own Father, making himself equal with God."

Acts 16:31-34 "They replied, 'Believe in the Lord Jesus, and you will be saved'... The jailer ... was filled with joy because he had come to believe in God."

1 Timothy 1:17 "Now to the King eternal, immortal, invisible, the only God, be honor and glory for ever and ever. Amen." See vs. 15-16 to identify as Jesus.

Titus 2:13 "while we wait for the blessed hope - the glorious appearing of our great God and Savior, Jesus Christ"

Hebrews 1:8 "But about the Son he says, 'Your throne, O God, will last for ever and ever, and righteousness will be the scepter of your kingdom.'"

Jesus is Lord and God:

John 20:28-29 "Thomas said to him, 'My Lord and my God!' Then Jesus told him, 'Because you have seen me, you have believed.'"

Jesus is Lord and Savior:

2 Peter 3:18 "But grow in the grace and knowledge of our Lord and Savior Jesus Christ. To him be glory both now and forever! Amen." Compare Isaiah 43:11 "I, even I, am the LORD (Yahweh), and apart from me there is no savior."

John 4:42 "...this man really is the Savior of the world."

Jesus is God over all:

Romans 9:5 "Theirs are the patriarchs, and from them is traced the human ancestry of Christ, who is God over all, forever praised! Amen."

Jesus is the true God, and eternal life:
> 1 John 5:20 "We know also that the Son of God has come and has given us understanding, so that we may know him who is true. And we are in him who is true - even in his Son Jesus Christ. He is the true God and eternal life."

Jesus is Alpha and Omega, First and Last, Beginning and End:
> Isaiah 44:6 "This is what the LORD (Yahweh) says -- Israel's King and Redeemer, the LORD Almighty: I am the first and I am the last; apart from me there is no God." Yahweh claims to be the greatest, the only God. Jesus claims the same: "I am the Alpha and the Omega, the First and the Last, the Beginning and the End" (Rev 22:13)

Jesus is The Lord of Glory:
> 1 Corinthians 2:8 "None of the rulers of this age understood it, for if they had, they would not have crucified the Lord of glory."

Jesus is Shepherd:
> Psalm 23:1 "The LORD (LORD=Yahweh) is my Shepherd."
> Now look:
> John 10:11,14 Jesus is the Good Shepherd.
> Hebrews 13:20 Jesus is the Great Shepherd.
> 1 Peter 5:4 Jesus is the Chief Shepherd.
> Rev 7:17 "The Lamb at the center of the throne will be their shepherd."

Jesus is King:
> Matt 25:31-46 "When the Son of Man comes in his glory, …he will sit on his throne in heavenly glory. …Then the King will say to those on his right…" Compare Isaiah 44:6 "This is what the Yahweh says: Israel's King" Also Psalm 10:16, 24:7; Is 44:6.

Jesus is the Holy One:
> Mark 1:24 "What do you want with us, Jesus of Nazareth? Have you come to destroy us? I know who you are — the Holy One of God!"
> John 6:69 "We believe and know that you are the Holy One of God."
> Rev 3:7 "These are the words of him who is holy and true" Compare these to Rev 16:5; 2 Kings 19:22; Psalm 22:3; Isaiah 40:25; Hosea 11:9.

3. Jesus has the same attributes of God:

Jesus has lived for all eternity:
>John 8:58-59 "'I tell you the truth,' Jesus answered, 'before Abraham was born, I am!' At this, they picked up stones to stone him" He called Himself Yahweh, which means, "Being One" or "Eternal One"
>John 17:5 "And now, Father, glorify me in your presence with the glory I had with you before the world began."
>Rev 22:13 "I am the Alpha and the Omega, the First and the Last, the Beginning and the End" Also Rev 1:8.

Jesus is unchanging:
>2 Timothy 2:13 "If we are faithless, he will remain faithful, for he cannot disown himself." (His character is unchanging. Much different than even angels!)
>Hebrews 1:10-12 "In the beginning, O Lord, you laid the foundations of the earth, and the heavens are the work of your hands. They will perish, but you remain; they will all wear out like a garment. ... But you remain the same, and your years will never end."
>Hebrews 13:8 "Jesus Christ is the same yesterday and today and forever."

Jesus is present everywhere:
>Matt 18:20 "For where two or three come together in my name, there am I with them." (Even angels and demons can only be in one place at a time.)

Jesus is all-knowing:
>Mark 2:8 "Immediately Jesus knew in his spirit that this was what they were thinking in their hearts, and he said to them, 'Why are you thinking these things?'"
>John 2:24-25 "But Jesus would not entrust himself to them, for he knew all men. He did not need man's testimony about man, for he knew what was in a man."
>John 6:64 "'Yet there are some of you who do not believe.' For Jesus had known from the beginning which of them did not believe and who would betray him."
>John 21:17 "Peter was hurt because Jesus asked him the third time, 'Do you love me?' He said, 'Lord, you know all things; you know that I love you.'"

Rev 2:23 "I will strike her children dead. Then all the churches will know that I am he who searches hearts and minds, and I will repay each of you according to your deeds."

Jesus is all-powerful:

Luke 8:25 "In fear and amazement they asked one another, 'Who is this? He commands even the winds and the water, and they obey him.'"

John 10:18 "No one takes it from me, but I lay it down of my own accord. I have authority to lay it down and authority to take it up again. This command I received from my Father."

John 2:19 "Jesus answered them, 'Destroy this temple, and I will raise it again in three days.'"

Hebrews 1:3 "The Son is the radiance of God's glory and the exact representation of his being, sustaining <u>all things</u> by his powerful word."

Philippians 3:20-21 "But our citizenship is in heaven. And we eagerly await a Savior from there, the Lord Jesus Christ, who, by the power that enables him to bring everything under his control, will transform our lowly bodies so that they will be like his glorious body."

Jude 9 "Even the archangel Michael, when he was disputing with the devil about the body of Moses, did not dare to bring a slanderous accusation against him, but said, 'The Lord rebuke you!'" Yet Jesus DID dare to rebuke the devil and the demons (Matt 16:23, 17:18, Mk 9:25, Lk 4:41)

Jesus has no sin:

John 8:46 "Can any of you prove me guilty of sin? If I am telling the truth, why don't you believe me?"

1 Peter 2:22 "He committed no sin, and no deceit was found in his mouth."

Jesus' throne is the same as God's throne:

Rev 22:1-5 "...the river of the water of life, as clear as crystal, flowing from the throne of God and of the Lamb ... The throne of God and of the Lamb will be in the city, and his servants will serve him. They will see his face, and his name will be on their foreheads."

Jesus is the same focus of worship as God, has the same glory as God:

Rev 21:22-23 "I did not see a temple in the city, because the
Lord God Almighty and the Lamb are its temple.
The city does not need the sun or the moon to
shine on it, for the glory of God gives it light, and
the Lamb is its lamp."

Jesus has the same priests serving him as serve God:

Rev 20:6 "The second death has no power over them, but they
will be priests of God and of Christ and will reign
with him for a thousand years."

Anyone that has seen Jesus has seen the Father:

John 1:15-18 "John testifies concerning him. He cries out,
saying, 'This was he of whom I said, 'He who
comes after me has surpassed me because he was
before me.' ... No one has ever seen God, but God
the One and Only, who is at the Father's side, has
made him known."

John 14:7-10 "If you really knew me, you would know my
Father as well. From now on, you do know him
and have seen him." Philip said, "Lord, show us
the Father and that will be enough for us." Jesus
answered: "Don't you know me, Philip?
...Anyone who has seen me has seen the Father.
How can you say, 'Show us the Father'? Don't you
believe that I am in the Father, and that the Father
is in me? The words I say to you are not just my
own."

Colossians 2:9 "For in Christ all the fullness of the Deity lives
in bodily form"

Jesus owns the angels:

Matt 13:41 "The Son of Man will send out his angels, and they
will weed out of his kingdom..." While in Luke
12:8 and 15:10 they are called the angels of God.

2 Thes 1:7 "...This will happen when the Lord Jesus is revealed
from heaven in blazing fire with his powerful
angels."

Jesus owns the church:

Matt 16:18 "...and on this rock I will build my church"

2 Thessalonians 1: 1-2 "...To the church of the Thessalonians
in God our Father and the Lord Jesus Christ:
Grace and peace to you from God the Father and
the Lord Jesus Christ."

Eph 5:24 "Now as the church submits to Christ, so also wives
should submit to their husbands in everything."

4. Jesus does things that only God can do:

Jesus created out of nothing:
> John 1:3-11 "Through him all things were made; without him nothing was made that has been made. ... He was in the world, and though the world was made through him, the world did not recognize him."
> Colossians 1:16 "For by him all things were created: things in heaven and on earth, visible and invisible, whether thrones or powers or rulers or authorities; all things were created by him and for him."

Jesus holds the world together:
> Colossians 1:17 "He is before all things, and in him all things hold together."
> Hebrews 1:3 "The Son is the radiance of God's glory and the exact representation of his being, sustaining all things by his powerful word."

Jesus is the Judge of all on Final Judgment Day:
> Matt 25:31-32 "When the Son of Man comes in his glory, ...he will sit on his throne in heavenly glory. All the nations will be gathered before him, and he will separate the people one from another" Compare to Joel 3:12 where Yahweh says, "there I will sit to judge all the nations on every side."
> John 5:22-23 "Moreover, the Father judges no one, but has entrusted all judgment to the Son."
> 2 Corinthians 5:9-10 "For we must all appear before the judgment seat of Christ, that each one may receive what is due him for the things done while in the body, whether good or bad."
> Jude 14-15 "See, the Lord is coming with thousands upon thousands of his holy ones to judge everyone, and to convict all the ungodly of all the ungodly acts they have done in the ungodly way."
> Rev 1:18 "I am the Living One; I was dead, and behold I am alive for ever and ever! And I hold the keys of death and Hades."

Jesus gives eternal life:
> John 14:6 "I am the way and the truth and the life. No one comes to the Father except through me."

John 10:28-30 "I give them eternal life, and they shall never perish; no one can snatch them out of my hand. My Father, who has given them to me, is greater than all; no one can snatch them out of my Father's hand. I and the Father are one." (The Jews then tried to kill him for blasphemy.)

John 5:21 "For just as the Father raises the dead and gives them life, even so the Son gives life to whom he is pleased to give it."

John 11:25-26 "Jesus said to her, 'I am the resurrection and the life. He who believes in me will live, even though he dies and whoever lives and believes in me will never die.'"

Jesus sends the Holy Spirit:

John 16:7 "But I tell you the truth: It is for your good that I am going away. Unless I go away, the Counselor will not come to you; but if I go, I will send him to you."

Acts 16:7 "They tried to enter Bithynia, but the Spirit of Jesus would not allow them to."

Phil 1:19 "I know that through your prayers and the help given by the Spirit of Jesus Christ, what has happened to me will turn out for my deliverance."

Jesus has the authority to forgive sins:

Matt 9:6-7 "But so that you may know that the Son of Man has authority on earth to forgive sins. . . ." Then he said to the paralytic, "Get up, take your mat and go home."

Jesus is directly and rightly prayed to:

Acts 7:55-60 "Stephen, full of the Holy Spirit, looked up to heaven ... Stephen prayed, 'Lord Jesus, receive my spirit.' Then he fell on his knees and cried out, 'Lord, do not hold this sin against them.'" We should pray to only the One True God (Mt 6:9, Ps 65:2, Isaiah 42:8).

Jesus places his own words on equal authority with God's words recorded in the Bible:

Matt 5:21-22 "You have heard that it was said to the people long ago, 'Do not murder' (Ex 20:13, given by the LORD/Yahweh), ... But I tell you that anyone who is angry with his brother will be subject to judgment."

Matt 5:27-28 "You have heard that it was said, 'Do not commit adultery.' (Ex 20:14, said by the LORD) But I tell you that anyone who looks at a woman lustfully has already committed adultery with her in his heart."

Matt 5:38-39 "You have heard that it was said, 'Eye for eye, and tooth for tooth.' (Ex 21:24) But I tell you, Do not resist an evil person. If someone strikes you on the right cheek, turn to him the other also."

Jesus demands to be followed and obeyed exclusively:

Luke 14:27 "Anyone who does not carry his cross and follow me cannot be my disciple."

John 21:22 "Jesus answered, 'If I want him to remain alive until I return, what is that to you? You must follow me.'" Also see Romans 14:6-12

5. Worship due only to God should be paid to Jesus:

All angels worship Jesus:
>Hebrews 1:6 "And again, when God brings his firstborn into the world, he says, 'Let all God's angels worship him.'" 1:14 says, "Are not all angels ministering spirits sent to serve those who will inherit salvation?" The point of Hebrews chapters 1&2 is that Jesus is greater than any angel.

Glory, power, honor, praise are given to Jesus:
>Rev 1:4-6 "...from Jesus Christ, who is the faithful witness, the firstborn from the dead, and the ruler of the kings of the earth. To him who loves us and has freed us from our sins by his blood, and has made us to be a kingdom and priests to serve his God and Father - to him be glory and power for ever and ever! Amen."

>Rev 5:11-12 "I looked and heard the voice of many angels, numbering thousands upon thousands, and ten thousand times ten thousand. ... In a loud voice they sang: 'Worthy is the Lamb, who was slain, to receive power and wealth and wisdom and strength and honor and glory and praise!'"

Jesus demands the **same honor** as God the Father:
>John 5:23 "that all may honor the Son just as they honor the Father. He who does not honor the Son does not honor the Father, who sent him."

Everyone in the universe will bow to Jesus and submit to him as Lord:
>Philippians 2:10-11 "that at the name of Jesus every knee should bow, in heaven and on earth and under the earth, and every tongue confess that Jesus Christ is Lord, to the glory of God the Father." (A quote from Isaiah 45:23)

Jesus accepts worship:
>Matthew 28:9-10 "They came to him, clasped his feet and worshiped him. Then Jesus said to them, 'Do not be afraid. Go and tell my brothers to go to Galilee; there they will see me.'"

>Luke 7:38 "...she began to wet his feet with her tears. Then she wiped them with her hair, kissed them and poured perfume on them."

John 9:38 "Then the man said, 'Lord, I believe,' and he worshiped him."

John 20:28 "Thomas said to him, 'My Lord and my God!'" Jesus did not correct him, and Jesus now commends Thomas' belief.

<u>Men are to be baptized **equally** into the name of Jesus, the Father, and the Holy Spirit:</u>

Matthew 28:19-20 "Therefore go and make disciples of all nations, baptizing them in the name of the Father and of the Son and of the Holy Spirit, and teaching them to obey everything I have commanded you. And surely I (Jesus) am with you always, to the very end of the age."

<u>Jesus is treated **equally** with the Father:</u>

John 14:23 "Jesus replied, 'If anyone loves me, he will obey <u>my</u> teaching. My Father will love him, and <u>we</u> will come to him and make our home with him.'"

2 Corinthians 13:14 "May the grace of the Lord Jesus Christ, and the love of God, and the fellowship of the Holy Spirit be with you all." (Also see Ephesians 1:2, Rev 1:4-5)

1 Thessalonians 3:11 "Now may our God and Father himself and our Lord Jesus clear the way for us to come to you."

Rev 5:13-14 "Then I heard every creature in heaven and on earth and under the earth and on the sea, and all that is in them, singing: 'To him who sits on the throne and to the Lamb be praise and honor and glory and power, for ever and ever!' The four living creatures said, 'Amen,' and the elders fell down and worshiped."

Rev 7:9-10 "I looked and there before me was a great multitude that no one could count, from every nation, tribe, people and language, standing before the throne and in front of the Lamb. ... And they cried out in a loud voice: 'Salvation belongs to our God, who sits on the throne, and to the Lamb.'"

Rev 11:15 "...loud voices in heaven, which said: 'The kingdom of the world has become the kingdom of <u>our Lord and of his Christ</u>, and he will reign for ever and ever.'"

To avoid error...

As you study each verse, look at surrounding words and paragraphs. This is called looking at the **"context."** If you pick out a verse blindly and ignore the context, you risk a wrong understanding of the passage. The verse with the main point is listed here, but in order to be sure you understand what it is saying, you must read before and after it.

Jesus declared that knowing Him was the same as knowing God (John 8:19), seeing Him was the same as seeing God (John 12:45), believing in Him was the same as believing in God (John 12:44), and receiving Him was the same as receiving God (Mark 9:37). The evidence is overwhelming. It is not only in one verse or in one book of the Bible. Jesus is more than a mere angel or spirit being or prophet or teacher. Jesus is "The Being One." The Creator. God come down in skin. Yahweh Himself. Isn't it time to turn to Him?

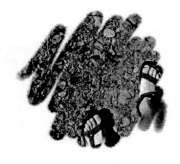

The Authors

Peter M. Denio is an associate pastor at Faith Baptist in Manchester, NH and holds a Masters degree in New Testament studies from Gordon-Conwell Theological Seminary. He is married to Cynthia, and they have 3 children. Peter has written devotional materials and curriculum (leader guides) for LifeWay Christian publishing. He is currently an elementary school teacher.

Contact: pcdenio@gmail.com ; (603) 641-5082
484 Vinton St., Manchester, NH 03103.

Daniel C. Lawry has a Masters of Divinity degree from Mid-America Baptist Theological Seminary in Schenectady, NY. He lives in Alplaus, NY, with his wife Angie and their seven children. Dan does fill-in preaching to help local pastors and does electrical engineering part time. He has directed Camp Pattersonville for the past 13 summers, teaching about 250 children there each year about the Lord Jesus. He also enjoys leading a Bible study at the Schenectady County Jail.

Contact: awldcl@juno.com ; (518) 399-5968
41 Hill St., Alplaus, NY 12008.

Notes

Made in the USA
Charleston, SC
09 December 2009